Downland
in
Flower

W. N. Macleod

S. B. Publications

First published in 2005 by S. B. Publications
Tel: 01323 893498
Email: sbpublications@tiscali.co.uk

ISBN 1-85770-310-3

Designed and Typeset by EH Graphics (01273) 515527

Contents

Acknowledgements

It is pleasant to introduce this book with heartfelt thanks to my family and friends.

Sarah, my wife, offered constructive criticism but, more importantly, by sharing my enthusiasms, she gave me great encouragement.

My good friend, Patrick Coulcher, has been a fount of knowledge. We have spent many happy days together on the Downs, searching for plants and butterflies.

My thanks, too, to Dennis Vinall for his help with plant identification.

I am also indebted to my friend, Janine Bland, for the time and care she devoted to the typing and retyping of the manuscript.

Dedicated to my mother, Priscilla, who led me, as a small boy,
through the wildflowers of Orkney and the Highlands

Introduction

I am fortunate to live on the very edge of Downland. A myriad of tracks take me to the hilltops, coombes, beechwoods, scrub and cliffs. A day's exertion brings me to Lewes and its environs: the western limit of "my" Downland.

Some fifteen years ago my work took me from Scotland to Sussex and in my initial forays on the chalk many of the plants were strange to me. I formed the idea of photographing the wild flowers within my walking orbit, keeping mainly on the chalk - as that is where I like to roam.

As my affection for this often gentle landscape grew I proceeded to photograph the plants, not as specimens but attempted to place them in the landscape, particularly amongst their fellow plants. The conjunction of different species, particularly if they flower simultaneously, can give great delight. Alternatively, I used a high power lens to capture particular aspects of a plant's design and colour which excited me. Consequently, while the wild flowers of this stretch of Downland by the sea are the focus of this essay, its arrangements are not conventional for a botanical work. I have made no attempt to be systematic and this is very much a personal anthology. Many commonly occurring local species have been omitted. There are, additionally, some interesting and rarer plants which I know to occur locally which I have not yet personally encountered - for example, Night-flowering Catchfly and Yellow Bird's-nest.

Beyond their beauty my interest in wild plants lies largely in their wildness - best if they grow in remote and quiet places. Like the people who have eaten them, used them, feared them, and loved them through the ages, they too have a history....

White Helleborine

May

Ivory spikes push through the accumulation of beech leaves which have sedimented, fall on fall. Shy of light, splashed yolk-yellow, and drawing paleness from the chalk, you will need to explore the margins of the wood to find them, set just in from the edge - White Helleborines - where brightness comes in moments, they stand dappled, hidden from the casual eye. A place where adders bask in clever camouflage. Throughout the South of England their habitat is dwindling and their numbers shrink. But here in Friston Forest, as the trees age and the leaf litter deepens, colonies expand and occupy new sites. Some spill exuberantly along shadowy woodland tracks. Just short of the great chalk cliffs, the Seven Sisters, is one of Britain's greatest beech woods, Friston Forest, with more than 4 million trees, now, after 80 years of growth, maturing as a rare plants' habitat. The hanger, the chalk beech wood, is a

White Helleborine

particular feature of Downland in West Sussex but in these eastern parts scrub and woods of Ash prevail. Scrub, dense with Hawthorn, with Elder and with Sloe. By the sea, the bareness of the heath is broken by banks of Privet and great clumps of Furze.

Some Helleborine colonies do extend several hundred metres into the forest to darker spots where the odd-looking Monotropa may flower in weeks to come. On the chalk banks of the forest rides the flowers of Germander Speedwell and Barren Strawberry mingle, roots entwined in a gentle union. Here, light floods in.

The egg-shaped flowers keep their shape, hanging off a knee-high spike. This flower is unusually opened, the yellow splash on its lower lip to entice the bees within. Andrena florea, the solitary bee, helps with pollination but insects are not necessary to the plant

Adder

Germander Speedwell and Barren Strawberry

Germander Speedwell

Wood Speedwell

Barren Strawberry

which is designed to self-pollinate - unlike many orchids it has a shrunken rostellum which allows pollen to fall directly on the stigma.

Culpeper [C] recommended an infusion of Speedwell leaves as a "provocative to venery and a strengthener" - indeed, the plant was taken as a cure for barrenness. Ironic that it lies abed with Barren Strawberry. Destroy the frail, trembling petals of the Speedwell at your peril - its white eye was the *Eye of Christ*. Or if not Christ's eye, *the Devil's eye!* Whatever, either God or the Devil will revenge any tampering. Alternatively, vengeful birds would be set upon your mother - hence *Pick-your-mother's-eyes-out* and, in Devon, retribution more violent yet - *Tear-your-mother's-eyes-out*. The folk names of many plants are of obscure origins, but some have been credited with plausible interpretations. Speedwell, an old fashioned term for goodbye, may have been a farewell token, suggested by its petals being taken on the breeze, and it may, too, have been a floral talisman for the traveller to keep him safe. Germander Speedwell's lowest petal is smaller than the others, and its stem quirky with hairs running down two opposing sides. Unlike Wood Speedwell, it has paired, unstalked leaves and from its heart-shaped fruit came another name - this the saddest of names - *Break-your-mother's-heart*.

Fuzzy stems and distinctive blue-green leaves of the Barren Strawberry readily distinguish it from Wild Strawberry, of a brighter green, which flowers later in the summer. No strawberry this strawberry, rather a Potentilla. And also a *Lazy-bones* - too lazy to fruit. Its fruit may disappoint but its flowers do not. Petals are widely spaced, delicate and white. They are framed by supporting green sepals, and in the heart of the flower is a round of orange nectaries - early nectar for both bumblebee and honeybee. It seems happy in compacted beech litter, then spilling from the wood and down its well-lit chalky banks - strange that such contrasting habitats suit it equally.

Bulbous Buttercup

On the open Downland slopes green goes to yellow with the unfolding of million upon million of bulbous buttercups. Cowslips and the Cow Parsley of late April and early May are displaced by blossom more extensive yet - brasher and brighter too. The close turf is coming into life, and many of the flowers that begin in May will flower on through summer. Salad Burnet would not look out of place anchored to the seabed with its tops swaying in the current. But its place is in the turf - on cliff-top, in the coombe and in clearings in the scrub. The heads are queer things, configured as green spheres, weird

Salad Burnet

sputniks. On each head red, sea anemone-like stigmas wave atop and purple stamens project below. As well as male and female flowers each inflorescence carries hermaphroditic flowers. It exploits the conditions of the cliff-top and the Downland summits with long and flexible filaments which fling pollen to the breeze. On wind-scoured spots it is kept short - but 8 cm - while in protected sites it will grow much taller.

Bright colours now fleck the turf: blues, yellows, whites, pinks, purples and reds as the milkworts, Fairy Flax, clovers, Dropwort, vetches and trefoils sense the start of summer. Salad Burnet grows freely in these parts and its handsome leaves lie all about the close-grazed sward. Those leaves have a strong cucumber scent and taste, can be put in salad, and in times past country folk used them to flavour home-brewed wine.

Dainty Herbs

Dainty milkworts and Fairy Flax show early in the season's parade of blossom: little pearly drops of white, pink, blue, lilac and magenta. Both are delicate, and both, happily, are commonplace. Fairly Flax's nodding buds open into tiny trumpets, and on the hotter days its petals splay

Common Milkwort

Chalk Milkwort

like Stitchwort. The structure of the Milkwort flower is contrastingly complex. Three small outer sepals are conventionally green while two prominent inner sepals envelop the petal tube. These casings or "wings", as they are called, are brightly coloured. The stamens are fused into a tube edged with a small petal on either side and a larger frilled petal on the underside. Milkwort flowers and flowers from spring to autumn. It is best for the traveller in these hills to come upon it as a creeping mat sharing a slope with other cheerful herbs.

Only the Common Milkwort has white flowers, but here, too, is the rarer Chalk Milkwort, of a different blue and with larger basal leaves. It extends beyond the South Downs and is seen, for example, on Salisbury Plain and in the Purbeck Hills.

The smallness of Fairy Flax does not, likely, relate to its name: in pre-Elizabethan times fairies were of human size. Its other name, *purging flax,* relates to its over-violent effect as a laxative. Milkwort had its uses too: initially as a Rogation Flower on the continent, and later given to nursing mothers to increase their flow of milk.

Fairy Flax

On exposed chalk Thyme and Rock-rose are putting on their buds. The Rock-rose has particularly beautiful buds - the colour of the petal shows through the bud casing while the lines along which the casing splits are marked in red. Both are track-side plants, particularly those tracks made by sheep and cattle

Rock-rose buds

that run along the terracettes of the northern scarp - there they grow in little hummocks, where winter's mud is hardened and the chalk shows through. If you stand on any downland top and

Rock-rose

see a chalk-white ribbon stretching into the distant haze, by it in the heat of summer will be the Rock-rose and the Thyme. Seeds of the Rock-rose germinate discontinuously, increasing their chances of survival. Some species on the other hand, eg, Small-flowered Buttercup, have seeds which germinate together.

A brave beauty on the cliff face, a wave of Thrift above the surging, milky tide, way, way down below. It has overcome excoriating winds and the scorching salt spray of winter gales to blossom and to put on seed. Rock falls, too, are a significant threat, but it likes the soft brown earth on the very cliff edge where the shelducks nest in abandoned rabbit holes. It uses water-saving strategies to survive: heads, a crush of papery petals, grow from dense and springy mats - one of its local names is *cushion pink* - which put down lengthy water-seeking roots. I

Cliff-top Thrift

have only seen it on the cliff-face, surprisingly not in the salt marsh at Cuckmere Haven. But it was from the salt marsh that it was taken and tamed for the city gentry to edge their flower beds. It is one of those rare native plants which found no place in the physic garden of the

Shelduck with young

Thrift

16th and 17th centuries - it was purely a plant to please the eye. It does grow inland in some parts of the country and, oddly, has a predilection for soil contaminated by metals such as copper or lead - hard to picture it blooming by a disused mine-shaft; no wheeling gulls, no crashing waves nor sharp horizon there.

Bluebells

Wind-torn leaves on the Stinking Iris attest to the harshness of the winter. But even here on the wind-whipped cliff the burst pods of the Iris will hold berries through to Christmas. Spring fetches up highly scented Bluebells and dainty Columbines to grace the cliff-top. Deeper in Downland the Bluebells inhabit the shade of Ash wood and Hazel coppice, where they bloom with *Weasel's Snout* and the Early Purple Orchid. Such small woods are scattered along the northern escarpment of the Downs as it falls sharply to the Weald. In the Weald itself the Bluebell woods are a notable feature, and in a well-managed Oak and Hornbeam wood run wide rivers of unending blue. Trampling the plant or removing its leaves will lead to its death by starvation although it will survive the removal of its flowering stem. In Scotland, it

Early Purple Orchids

Yellow Archangel

Ramsons

is the *wild hyacinth*, the name my mother used: in the Highlands they grow by fast-flowing rivers with glinting Birch bark as their foil. The presence of Early Purple Orchids on the cliff-top indicates there was once a cover of woodland: a meagre vestige of an earlier, now long-gone, ecology. Strangely, country folk gave the Bluebell and the Early Purple the same name - sometimes it was *snake's head,* sometimes *adder's flower* - suggesting those plants were invested with sexual power. Gerard[G] had the Bluebell's root "full of slimie glewish juice". They stored a magic, equal in force, piercing the ground together, blossoming together and finally wilting together. Pale anthers, muted clappers, kept in its dark-striped bell. But this plant had no mention in the herbals until William Turner's "The Names of Herbs" (1548): it was unknown to the ancient cultures of the Mediterranean being native only to the Atlantic coastlands. The glue it yielded, which can be got simply from chewing the bulb, was used by little boys "to set feathers upon arrows and to paste books with" [G]. It gave, too, a starch grand for stiffening Elizabethan ruffs - the *"best starch next to cuckoo pint"* [G]. Our Bluebell, Hyacinthoides non-scriptus - unlettered - has no inscription of regret upon its petals. The original, and mythical, hyacinth grew from the spilt blood of Hyacinthus, accidentally killed by Apollo. Moved in grief Apollo marked it with the word "alas". Under the Ash they grow with *Weasel's Snout.*

Yellow, gashed with red, as entrancing as any orchid, its scent is the stink of weasel. In shady spots where Ramsons like to rule, Yellow Archangel grows on track-sides, where Moschatel has been and Sanicle will follow.

Leaves splashed by the blood of Christ, nectar-filled spurs, aphrodisiacal tubers and seeds like dust - known in Sussex as *ramshorn*, in Scotland as *puddock's spindles* (kite legs), elsewhere as the *cross flower* - a crucifixion plant - this is the Early Purple Orchid. This, the first orchid to be described by Dioscorides - Kunosorchis - the dog testicle. Food is stored in the two oval tubers, one full, yet to give up its energy for the next year's growth, the other flaccid and shrinking, drained by current growth and fruiting. According to Dioscorides the tubers were taken in goat's milk, the full one to fire up lust and the slack one to restrain it. Alternatively if a man ate the fat tuber he would father a male child while if a woman ate the smaller one she would bear a daughter. The down-to-earth country folk of Forfarshire called it *"bull's bag"*, and in the sixteenth century it was taken as a generator of sperm. Robert Turner had it that as many orchids as were needed to pleasure all the seamen's wives in Rochester grew in Croham Park in Kent. It likes lime-rich soil and is pollinated by the Buff-tailed Bumblebee, Bombus Terresteris. Tall in woodland and necessarily stunted on the cliff-top, its spike may hold as many as fifty flowers each with a three-lobed labellum. A beauty, no matter that it stinks of tomcat's urine. It can remain in a vegetative state for many years, then burst into flower when scrub is cleared or woods are felled. It puts on flower as early as mid-April and is the first Downland orchid of the year. Like the Fragrant Orchid, and other plants that we will meet, it can make blossoms that are unsullied white.

Early Purple Orchid

Bird's-foot Trefoil is a caterpillar food plant for the Common Blue and the Green Hairstreak. Here a male alights to take its nectar. Usually seen in numbers, whether feeding or flying, they overnight head down, aligned head-to-tail on the stems of grasses. A ubiquitous delight, this Trefoil puts colour on the turf, dry chalk banks, pastures and the shingle beach. Its flowers, some with dramatic red streaks, have the typical pea-family structure and there may be six in a head. Its generic name, lotus, means three-leaved, despite a further pair of leaflets, quite divorced from the trefoil. With buds still shut, stamens swell taking the pollen to the stigmas. It seems this plant gives more to insects than it takes - and even with Clover growing all about it bees may work it preferentially. The pods and flowers have striking features, and so a plethora of folk names. The elongated pods suggest claws, either of the crow or the Devil. In many countries the bright trefoil was associated with the goblin Tom Thumb - so took his name.

Common Blue on Bird's-foot Trefoil

Sprouting *devil's claws* it was evidently a plant to be wary of, but not all of its associations were malign: country humour also had it as *grandmother's toenails.*

A great shingle bank plugs a short gap in the cliffs at Cuckmere Haven. In May pale shoots stir the shingle and shortly a forest of Sea Kale appears, as if from nowhere. Like Sea Lavender it produces a good flow of nectar but neither grows in sufficient abundance to excite the beekeeper. Once common on Sussex shores, it is now infrequent - probably through over-vigorous harvesting. Elsewhere it grows in sand, and spring shoots can be blanched by heaping sand or shingle on them, then the white stems and yellow leaves can be cut for table use. It was popularised as a vegetable in the 18th century when large amounts were taken off the shores, loaded into carts and transported to the seaside market towns and later on to London. It spreads its seed in a buoyant pod that is taken by the tide. Sophisticated adaptive designs permit some species to sow their seed on water where it can remain buoyant for up to six

Sea Kale

months - giving a good chance of effective dispersal. The seed-coat of the Yellow Iris, for example, incorporates air-containing tissues.

Below the turf the herbs' roots bunch and cross, hence its elasticity. Some plants have long tap roots designed to seek out moisture from the driest chalk while others parasitise by locking roots to steal from other plants. Yellow Rattle is such a drought cheater: a characteristic plant of the chalk

Yellow Rattle

grassland which blooms early and flowers through high summer. The two vivid ink-blue teeth on its upper lip may serve as a signal to the bumblebee. On the underside of its leaves, apparent through a hand lens, are pores - hydathodes - which excrete any surplus water. Despite the mint-like features - opposite pairs of leaves, tubular two-lipped flowers and a square stem - it is from the figwort family. The generic Rhinanthus (nose flower) refers to the shape of its petal.

Through early summer it blossoms with

Horseshoe Vetch, Bird's-foot Trefoil, Restharrow and Wild Mignonette. Later with Dropwort, Centaury, clovers and Viper's Bugloss. Before intensive farming methods were introduced its black-speckled stems were rife in grassy meadows. In this area it grows prolifically just in from the cliff edge under the ripple of tall grasses. Its inflated calyx is the palest of pale greens which, when filled with ripe seed, forms the rattle to be

shaken by the summer breeze. The dry capsules are otherwise known as fiddle-cases, or in Scotland as *gowk's siller* - fool's silver.

In the remote denes of Caburn the Burnt Orchid enjoys seclusion - a tiny orchid under an arcing sky. This is a fine tramp along the chalk from Eastbourne. Follow the thin white ribbon which dips, twists and, after stretching endlessly, disappears in the blue of distance. Travel in the third week of May when the plants will be in flower and the Skylarks trill. Elsewhere, late-flowering forms will share the turf with a different set of neighbours; Rock-rose, Ploughman's Spikenard and Marjoram. But now it sits among the yellows of the Horseshoe Vetches, the reds of Sorrels and the creamy froth of Dropworts and of Hawthorn.

Sussex holds the largest population of Burnt Orchids in Britain, with the greatest concentration of sites between Eastbourne and Lewes. Most colonies are modest with less than fifty spikes, with the occasional exception. Kent has only May-flowering plants, and in Derbyshire, where

Burnt Orchid

it is very rare, it grows on limestone grassland. Its flower buds are dark maroon, rather like those of Marjoram, hidden by its purplish bracts. In the early form its hood starts dark and fades to white as the flower opens leaving a dark crown on a pale spike. In the late flowering plants (July) the dark hood keeps its colour, rendering a different overall effect. Usually ankle high, it likes well-drained, undisturbed slopes of ancient grassland. It needs lime about its roots, and if lime is absent certain minerals, such as aluminium, are more soluble and act as a poison to the plant. The first record of this orchid in Sussex, from the Downs at the back of Eastbourne, was in the year of the French Revolution. A specimen picked in Jevington in the year of Trafalgar can still be seen in William Borrer's herbarium, now in Kew. Borrer's

father was the High Sheriff in Sussex when the Napoleonic War was raging. Father and son made frequent passages across the Downs on horseback to provision troops on the Sussex coast. By these sorties he came in touch with the plants of Downland. His initial delight then became a passion and, ultimately, he was one of Sussex's greatest botanists.

The Small Blue, small indeed, depends on Kidney Vetch to feed its caterpillar. But it takes a strong insect, likely a Bumblebee, to prise open the flowers of this vetch to drink its nectar and plunder its pollen. With the act of union done, the calyces expand to form an attractive pale and woolly head. Unlike Bird's-foot Trefoil its pods are not crow's feet, toes, nor claws but simple egg-shapes. Extensive colonies can dominate eroding banks, carpet Downland slopes and creep from chalk onto the shingle. In these parts I have only ever seen it yellow but there are five distinct sub-species in the United Kingdom, some red, some whitish and some, even, purplish.

Kidney Vetch

As spring goes to summer a torrent of white blossom spills across the Downs, the scrub lights up, the hedgerows are effulgent: these weeks of white on green are pure delight. A time for wandering and wondering. Country folk believed that May was a month when supernatural forces were at their height and used the Hawthorn as a defence against the sinister - the Rowan was used in a similar way in Scotland and Ireland. Also a promoter of fertility, a symbol of growth and of renewal. Branches would be taken from the May-tree and woven into circles and crosses to enhance the

Hawthorn

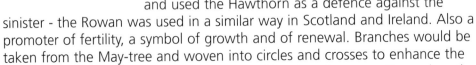

Hawthorn's power. These days the flowering of the May usually occurs no earlier than the second week of the month (since the last calendar change of 1732) - too late to usher in the month. But in 2004 it opened earlier - in time to work its Mayday magic. So important a day that the Irish believed the sun rose early. Its scent has undertones of sex and decay: the flowers contain trimethylamine, an ingredient of the sweet smell of putrefaction making the blossom attractive to carrion-insects which became its pollinators. It was long held that the blossom retained and gave off the stench of the "Great Plague". Conversely, it contains amigdalin, an appealing and delicious constituent of almond. Good years are few and far between, but when Hawthorn generates a good nectar flow its heady fragrance can be detected in the hive. Like other plants of magic it had a dangerous side and was not entirely benign - the *hag-bush* was never to be disturbed: cut it down and it would bleed, just as Christ's head bled, crowned by this very thorn. Other plants, too, at this time work their magic - farmers used the rub of a Buttercup on the cow's udder to coax more milk.

Through the winter a sticky coating has protected the Horse Chestnuts' buds. Earlier in spring honeybees took it to make their propolis. Bees embalm - any intruder, perhaps an ill-starred mouse, will be stung to death then embalmed in propolis to prevent decomposition. This reddish resin they also use as "bee glue" to close small gaps. In spring bees working these trees look as though they have had brick dust sprinkled on their backs. Now the trees are stacked with candles - not simply white, but suffused by corals, apricots and reds. The nectar guides on the petals are at first yellow but later redden.

Horse Chestnut

I was surprised when I first walked the cliffs at Beachy Head to see the nodding heads of Columbine. But here it is, dark blue or palest pink in the shadow of the Wayfaring Tree, only a stone's throw from the cliff's white face. Like many other buttercups, *granny's nightcap* is poisonous, but its charms were nicely captured by Gerard's description: "with five little hollowe horns as it were hanging foorth, with small leaves standing upright the shape of little birds". Its glittering black seed was taken in wine to bring "a speedy delivery of women in childbirth" [C].

Columbine

Inland, the Wayfaring Tree grows as scrub with Elder, Sloe and Privet. It also grows abundantly along the downland tracks, often hung with Honeysuckle and with Bryony. It was named by Gerard from its abundance along southern chalkland ways. Like the Privet, it is a chalk-dwelling shrub and white-flowered. Also known as *shepherd's delight*, for it was a useful tree to countrymen - its roots were made into bird-lime, which was used to catch small birds, its leaves boiled in lye gave a black hair dye, its pliant twigs were used to tie

Wayfaring Tree

bundles and to make fast gates. As well as fastening gates the plant was used medicinally to fasten loosened teeth.

The Privet on the cliff grows in great dense clumps, wind-sculpted by the prevailing westerlies. Its aerodynamic forms rise and fall above the rise and fall of the Seven Sisters.

Ramping through the Blackthorn and the Hawthorn scrub, Black Bryony is most apparent in the winter when chains of glossy bright red berries dangle in the gloom. But in bloom its spikes of miniature, washed-out flowers are easily overlooked. More likely to be noticed are its large, pointed leaves with their unique plasticky gloss. Some creepers twine clockwise, others scramble

Wayfaring Tree

anticlockwise: Black Bryony is a clockwise twiner and dioecious - male and female flowers found on different plants. In woodland it forsakes the Honeysuckle and the Hawthorn for the company of pale orchids. The white flowers of the Greater Butterfly Orchid are green-tinged, exotic, with trailing lips and spurs. A rare orchid in this area, it is more prevalent in the beech hangers of West Sussex. There it is also known in chalk pasture.

Black Bryony clasps an orchid

Alas, I have never seen it hereabouts in open Downland. Its sweet scent is mainly for the night when its pollinators, the long-tongued, night-flying moths visit it for nectar. The nectar level is visible through the wall of the downcurving spur. The Elephant Hawk Moth is one such pollinator and it feeds, too, off Honeysuckle. Woodland clearings, with stands of Willowherb, are its breeding ground: the Willowherbs are the main food plants of its caterpillar which, for a defence, has striking false eyes, and the ability to retract its head if being attacked. The tubers of the Greater Butterfly Orchid are tapering rather than ovoid, and like other orchids, it can be vegetative for years, then reappear with the clearance of established woodland.

Elephant Hawk Moth caterpillar

The Lesser Butterfly Orchid, more widespread nationally, growing on acid soils in the north, is not found here.

Black Bryony comes

from a tuber which, like its berries, is poisonous unless boiled. Spring shoots used to be cooked as a vegetable, while the berries have been known to kill cattle. This is the only native British yam, a family of mostly tropical plants with edible tubers. Gerard made the earliest English record of Black Bryony. Dioscorides recommended it to remove freckles and bruises: so good was it for taking off a bruise that the French called it "l'herbe aux femmes battues" - the herb for battered wives.

Greater Butterfly Orchid

Once the spring nectar supplies of Sycamore and Dandelion are exhausted, White Clover is one of the first downland plants to produce "main-flow" nectar for the bees. It grew well, too, on the slag heaps of the Black Country where enterprising beekeepers put it to good use. Its scent was made in heaven. Not only farmers and beekeepers take from it: Orange Tips sip from it early in the year while the rarer Clouded Yellow also has an affinity with clover later on. Red Clover florets have particularly long corolla tubes and not all species of honeybee have probosces long enough to reach their nectar, unless a heavy dew can bring the level up.

White Clover

The somewhat sinister Broomrape is most often seen on clover. The roots of clover are nodular and hold symbiotic bacteria which are capable of fixing nitrogen. The nodules are tinged pink by haemoglobin which, like human haemoglobin, has a high affinity for oxygen and sequesters it. Nitrogenase, the enzyme which fixes nitrogen, can then function as it needs an anaerobic atmosphere. Strange to think we share haemoglobin with the plants. The 'rape' of Broomrape is its globular root, or turnip, not its ravishing of the clover: a root once candied in the country kitchen. Its spread through dairy pastures may relate, at least in part, to contaminated agricultural clover seed. The smaller-flowered, cliff-top forms here on England's very southern edge are likely to be the most native forms of clover. It sports a delicate white "eyebrow" at the base of each leaflet and when fertilised its flowers flop - perhaps just one will be left standing - *old maid* to country children.

Clouded Yellow

Broomrape

All of Broomrape's nourishment comes from its host so it has no need of chlorophyll. Of our twelve native Broomrapes most are rare and hard to distinguish. I usually come upon an isolated spike rather than a colony. Ivy

Horseshoe Vetch

Adonis Blue mating

Broomrape is mainly coastal in the South West of England and Southern Ireland. Thyme Broomrape is very local in Western Scotland and the Outer Hebrides. Knapweed may also be parasitised, but rarely on these hills - Glyndebourne is the place to look. Despite the prevalence of Oxtongue only very rarely does it act as a host: there are only six localities where it has been seen, spread around Sussex, Kent and the Isle of Wight. In Kent there is a Broomrape living off wild carrot.

As with Bird's-foot Trefoil, Horseshoe Vetch takes its name from its seed pods: these consist of horseshoe-shaped segments which spring apart when the seeds are ripe and ready for ejection. It is an important plant to Downland butterflies. The most intense blue of any of our butterflies belongs to the Adonis Blue which in later summer feeds from Knapweed but now its nectar source is Horseshoe Vetch. It lays eggs singly on the underside of the vetch's leaf in May and again in August: so there are two generations, one from the later yellow-striped caterpillar which hibernates through winter to fly in May, the other, from the earlier eggs, flies in August. The caterpillar of the silvery-blue Chalkhill Blue also feeds off it: another butterfly of the chalk pasture restricted to the Downs and other warm limestone hills such as the Cotswolds and the Chilterns. When a bee settles on its golden lip, the plant puts out a puff of pollen. Doused in the pale dust, it hovers to probe this bloom, then that one and another, ensuring that more seed will fill the horseshoe; then more of its pale gold will tumble down dry chalk banks where Thyme and Bastard Toadflax lie. Exuberant - see it cascade over the sheer slopes of a disused chalk pit, a crumbling cliff or a steeply-cut bostal bank, where later follow Yellow-wort and, at summer's end, spirals of dainty Lady's-tresses.

Even on the cliff-top many micro-habitats sit side by side: a rabbit scrape, an anthill, a fissure on the cliff edge, chalk rubble, the lee of a privet 'aerofoil': all provide varying levels of shelter from the scorch of salt spray, sun and wind.

A close inspection of the cliff's very edge yields some fine reward. Stony scrapes and threadbare turf are ideal for a mat of Common Storksbill. Its fern-like leaves and pink-purple petals please, but it is the striping of the sepals and the beaking of the fruit capsules which are so unusual. It keeps close to the ground and needs to be viewed at sod level to be appreciated. The

Common Storksbill

Beaked fruit capsules

White form

Storksbills form a group which is difficult to separate: several are in dwarf form in coastal turf. Sea Storksbill has toothed oval leaves and rarely puts on petals. Normally its leaves are softly hairy but by the sea they are sometimes sticky: likely for added protection. It is a much more local species, distributed along the Sussex coast to the Scillies and along the West Coast of England to the Solway. On our cliffs it has but a single site.

Exposed to identical conditions is the Green-winged Orchid. It, too, has striped sepals. It takes its name from the splendid green veining which ornaments its hood. Orchids in such an exposed setting tend to be small in comparison with those that grow inland, often in the protection offered by a churchyard. Before the Second World War it was a common Sussex orchid, but after drainage and the ploughing of the damp meadows much of its habitat vanished. Most sites in East Sussex are on the Weald and I have only ever seen it on one cliff-top.

Green-winged Orchid

In damper places, where soils are heavier, Yellow Rocket and Cut-leaved Crane's-bill are now in flower. Spouts of yellow flame burst from the rolling meadows at the foot of the escarpment. The latter, in hedgebanks and in pastures, is small-flowered and more noteworthy for its dramatic leaf.

Yellow Rocket

The French call it *hangman*, otherwise its split labellum makes it a snake's forked tongue - *adder's tongue*. Twayblade growing on open slopes flowers much earlier than in woodland. Under the Hazel it stands - now half-lit, then in a ray of light - by the Butterfly Orchid, and on the chalk amongst burgeoning humps of Marjoram. One hundred little waxy men may hang on a single spike, which beetles will climb upon to steal their nectar. And when this goal is reached sticky pollen is fired over the head of any innocent insect that touches its explosive rostellum. Frightened by the sudden jet of pollen the insect flees the plant: just as nature intended and so to fertilise another.

Cut-leaved Crane's-bill

Twayblade

Sanicle

Burnet Rose

As a failsafe it can also propagate by budding off its spreading root.

Back in a copse, or shaw, usually amongst Sycamore and Ash shy Sanicle can now be found. Twayblade's leaves are striking but not beautiful, whilst Sanicle's are amongst the loveliest - "finely dented about the edges" [C]. In the Middle Ages Sanicle was a wound healer par excellence. A typical wound drink contained Bugle, Yarrow and Sanicle: the first to hold the wound open, the second to cleanse it and then Sanicle to heal it. The French called it "herbe de St Laurent" after St Lawrence, a Christian martyr who was grilled to death on a gridiron - naturally it became the plant for treating burns.

Spinosissima, the spiniest rose, or pimpinellifolia from the close resemblance of its leaf to the Burnet Saxifrage: the Burnet Rose - with red stalks, pure white flowers and hips almost livid, blue-black, like great drops of venous blood oozing from its stems. Above the cliff its flowers hug the ground, some seemingly stalkless - strangely sessile for a rose. How unexpected, these beautiful blossoms scattered on the ground. In amongst the scrub, in clearings protected from the wind, floral carpets close-woven with Milkwort, Horseshoe Vetch, Tormentil, Salad Burnet, Heath Speedwell and Dropwort share the shelter with Burnet Rose to grow in secret - wild gardens of delight in which to pause a while.

The cliff-top soils are dry, much to the liking of Heath Speedwell, so here it proliferates, particularly on slopes in the lee of the wind. The species name, officinalis, indicates that it was stocked by apothecaries. For example, it was given in the treatment of tuberculosis. Otherwise, *speed-you-well*, a spray of its blossom pinned to the traveller's breast to protect against misfortune. The genus, Veronica, may have been dedicated to the saint said to have wiped Christ's feet on his way to the cross on Calvary. As the Burnet Rose breaks bud, Dropwort is no more than a bead of white, tinged coral pink - but a bud still lovelier than the blossom it contains. But these are not its drops, its drops are hidden in the shallow soil; roots swollen here and there into pea-sized tubers. It is a Downland signature plant and it is rare to find it off the chalk - on dry, calcareous grassland on the Yorkshire Wolds, for example, and, unexpectedly, in the alien habitat of the Lizard. The cliff-top form is short but its flowers dance just above the smallest May-time herbs. Deep in the Downs away from the Channel gales, grown taller, Dropworts sway in drifts amongst the Sorrel and the lanky grasses. Sheep's Fescue and Red Fescue are our common Downland grasses but two sedges, Spring Sedge, and the later and taller Carnation Grass, catch the traveller's eye. If the slopes are under-

Heath Speedwell

Dropwort

grazed such tall, rank grasses as Tor-grass and False Brome dominate and exclude the dainty herbs.

Scented, small and yellow, the cruciform flowers of Crosswort are stacked in whorls on a long and hairy stem. This soothing wound herb [C] was first described by Gerard on a botanising trip to the village of Hampstead where he found it in the churchyard. It tends to grow in limey spots, sometimes out of spoil about

Spring Sedge

the entrances to foxes' holes and badgers' setts. It is well represented on Lullington Heath, where its clumps are scattered amongst Wood Sage. Sheep's Sorrel is less flamboyant than its taller relative, Common Sorrel, is an acid-lover and certainly a lime-hater - but on Lullington Heath it finds a refuge from surrounding chalk. It grows in close-bound groups which shimmer as the plants dance and have the summer breeze

Dropwort

transport their pollen. Sorrel is from the old French "surele" meaning sour, the taste of its leaf. It was one of many antiscorbutic remedies - Scurvy Grass, Cochlearia officinalis, another from the apothecary's shelf, is a foreshore plant, a cabbage not a grass, used by early mariners for its vitamin C to protect against the scurvy.

Furzy spots are good for bird life - the Stonechat often perches on the furze to sing its scratchy song - but gorse scrub needs constant clearing as it is so quick-growing and invasive. There are definite advantages to its presence but it

Common Sorrel

Crosswort

Glorious Furze

needs to be carefully controlled. Its roots are virtually indestructible: burn it to the ground and within days new growth will appear. There is usually a flush of flowering in December, however not on a scale to compare with the yellow blaze of May. Lie on a grassy slope downwind of a bank of furze and be intoxicated by the heady smell of coconut. The Linnet likes to make its nest a few feet off the ground - furze and bramble are well suited - and later in the year it feeds amongst the corn stubble of adjacent fields.

Quick draining chalk seems an unlikely habitat for screeds of glossy buttercups but the Bulbous Buttercup, the first of its kind to flower, will not brook flooding and loves these Downland slopes. As Culpeper said, "they grow everywhere, unless you run your head into a hedge you cannot but see them as you walk". It is a characteristic plant of dry, rich grassland. Anemonil in its sap makes it a blister plant - the whole plant is poisonous: malign drifts of yellow left quite alone by bees.

Strangely, the pollen of some buttercups is also injurious to bees. Its blistering capacity was its signature. Therapeutic cupping, or blistering, was widely used in the Middle Ages to remove ill humours from the body. It was a drawer of poisons as well as a poison in its own right: a poultice for the bubae of the plague. Also *crazyweed* - hung about the neck "of him that is lunatike in the wane of the moon", able to return him to sanity. Growing from a globular corm and having reflexed sepals it is set apart from the Meadow and Creeping Buttercups. Sorrel in its early flowering is a companion of the Bulbous Buttercup, and a plant of which extensive use was made. Its applications were legion; a thirst quencher, a tobacco, a salad, a stain remover and a pot

Bulbous Buttercup

herb. Marching Roman soldiers sucked the leaves to ease their thirst. In Tudor times it was a highly valued vegetable, the sour bite of its leaves enjoyed in sauces, much as we use lemon. Linen was rescued from rust and ink stains. Whether gypsies really did smoke it? - likely they did as one of its folk names was *gypsies baccy*.

Sheep's Sorrel

Between Seaford Head and Beachy Head is the greatest concentration of Early Spider Orchid in Sussex. This rare and local orchid is found only in Dorset, Wiltshire, Kent and Sussex, confined to about thirty localities. The earliest herbarium specimen is in the Kew collection, from Birling Gap (1837). Its labellum, furry like its pollinating bee, is franked with a silver H. It has been recorded on Lullington Heath but I have not seen it there in recent years. There are twelve populations along the coast from Seaford to Beachy Head. Rarer still is the Late Spider Orchid, confined to some ten localities on the North Downs and East Kent.

Early Spider Orchid

One of the loveliest grasses pushing through the Buttercup slopes is the Quaking Grass, with its hair-thin stems and its shivering heads - it is also known as *shivering grass*. Its dearth of foliage makes it useless as a fodder but adds to its attraction.

A sweet hay-scented mattress stuffing, the yellow Bedstraw, on which the Virgin Mary gave birth to baby Christ - hence the claim that its use guaranteed safe confinement. In France Beech leaves were used as a mattress filler for so-called "talking beds": such was the noise they made. Not all sanitising herbs were so fragrant - pungent Mugwort was burned to cleanse the sickroom. Lady's Bedstraw was thought to dispel fleas, specifically. Culpeper used it, "stuffed up the nostrils" to stay nose bleeds. Ironically, it contains coumarin, which as dicoumarol is an anticoagulant: scarcely likely to

Late Spider Orchid

Early Spider Orchid

Quaking Grass

Lady's Bedstraw

Broom

benefit a nose bleed. While it stops blood curdling, it was used to curdle milk: a substitute for rennet - hence its moniker *cheese rennet*. Food for the caterpillar of the Broad Bordered Bee Hawk Moth, whose transparent wings aid its mimicry of the bee. And a dye plant - yellow coaxed from leaf and red from root. The effect of soil pH on the competition between species has been studied in the Bedstraws. Some plants which are calcicolous in the wild will grow in lime-deficient soil, and some calcifuges will grow in lime-rich soil - as long as they are not subject to competition. Heath Bedstraw normally found on acid heaths, will grow well on chalky soil, but if a calcicolous Bedstraw is introduced it will be overwhelmed by its lime-loving relative.

Broom's rich scent is absent from these hills, but it does grow in Abbot's Wood below the scarp. Picked from claggy rides and the banks of woodland streams, Bugle was the *"carpenter's herb"*. Carpenters, with their exposure to the saw and the adze, were prone to cuts and Bugle was used to staunch their bleeding. Associated with the Oak, there it will flower "in shadowie places[G]" till mid-summer. Seen here in waterlogged clay, it creeps across the

Bugle

ground pencilling a delicate blue pattern on the grass. Beyond its two-lipped flower extend blue stamens, while its minty leaves take on a glossy darkening, going to strange shades of brown, green and purple. Culpeper sang its praises: "keep a syrup of it always by you" - just as we would have an aspirin in our bathroom cabinet, he gave a convincing description of delirium tremens: "such as give themselves much to drinking are troubled with strange fancies, strange sights in the night and some with voices" and recommended this herb, having, supposedly, a mild narcotic effect. He also applied it to "such ulcers and sores as happen in the secret parts of men and women": likely a combination of venereal diseases and genital cancers. By it spreads frilly Lousewort, a pretty wee thing, and nice with Tormentil.

Pignut stands frail and wavering, now in sunshot and now in gloom, above Bluebell leaves splayed flaccid and near defunct on the

Lousewort

woodland floor. Elsewhere in the wood the Pignuts share a grassy bank with Yellow Pimpernel, Wild Strawberry, Bugle and Wood Spurge - just the place for a *fairy potato* of Irish folklore. It is starchy, "the earth nut" - like a truffle - and pigs were used to smell them out.

Pignut

In boggy woodland places Ragged Robin grows by Lesser Stitchwort and Yellow Iris. Such places are found along the Cuckmere as it meanders though the Downs and in woods below the northern scarp. The Yellow Iris, (*flags* to my mother, *water flags* to Gerard, *Fleur de Lys* to Louis VII), was an apotropaic plant like Ragged Robin. And a plant of the wet: claggy places soaked in Highland drizzle where black-faced sheep shelter in roofless crofts - there it flowers, often to spectacular effect, with the Rhododendron and the Rowan. See it and Ragged Robin not in swampy southern woodland ditches, rather in the bogs of Orkney and the margins of its shallow lochs where they abound amongst Marsh Orchids, Myrtle and waving Cotton Grass. There is where it belongs, not in dank stagnant pools at Downland's edge, definitely not behind the sweep of Seaford's shingle. Pick it at your peril: it is a thunder plant. The peril in Lesser Spearwort is in the sap - sap that can kill sheep and cattle. Duplicitous beggars looking for sympathy and alms would fill an empty limpet shell with the pulp of the plant, then press it into the skin to manufacture weals.

The Cuckmere valley, which cuts north-south through these chalk hills, is an excellent habitat for aquatic and water-meadow plants, and later in the year some of the most beautiful of Downland's plants will flower here - Flowering Rush, Arrowhead and Frogbit. Now we can savour the delicious blue of Brooklime, the mud-loving speedwell. A valued plant: its leaves rich in vitamin C for salad, a poultice for inflamm-ations, and an abortifacient in stillbirth. Its

Ragged Robin

Yellow Pimpernel

Yellow Iris

Lesser Stitchwort

Brooklime

Lesser Spearwort

likeliest home in these parts is a marshy clearing in an ancient copse.

On the Levels, Reed buntings fly fast above the drainage ditch, a wing burst then a glide - reminiscent of the Yaffle, but altogether sharper, full of urgency. A Moorhen jumps from her reed-thatched nest sending a ripple across the whisky-coloured water to rock the Water Violets.

Unlike the Early Spider Orchid and Early Purple Orchid, the Common Spotted shoots from finger-like tubers not from "fox stones". Like the Marsh Orchid it is a Dactylorchid and found throughout the country. Its spikes are dense, its flower slender and untapered. Usually its leaves are spotted but there is a white form with unmarked leaves. As with Twayblade, the woodland plants flower later than those on open sites. On the Weald it grows and hybridises with the clay-loving Heath Spotted Orchid (a plant not seen on the chalk). A flowery hollow I like to visit at this happy time of year sports Twayblade, Spotted Orchid and Grass Vetchling blossoming side by side. A handsome crimson flower, the *crimson shoe* - this was the name suggested by Geoffrey Grigson, and a good one, too.

Water Violet

Common Spotted Orchid

A pea masquerading as a grass, whose "leaves" are of great botanical interest as they are flattened leaf stalks - phyllodes. It lacks "true" leaf blades as does the sombre Butcher's Broom. Often found near the sea, indeed it grows at Beachy Head, it is not averse to the chalk but it is more likely on neutral soils. The South East of England is

where it is mostly found, but it does extend north to Lincolnshire and west to Devon. Elegant, sparse, shapely: quite fabulous. More prosaic is its cousin, the Meadow Vetchling, a cheerful scrambler and a universal plant. Its heads are a lively yellow and its stems are square. A weed, for once, a friend of the farmer, being a nitrogen fixer. In ancient pasture it would have been welcome as it enhances the nutritional value of hay. One of its country names is *yellow tare-tine* - "tare" an old name for vetch, and like most vetches it is an important plant to caterpillars.

Brownwort from the colour of its queer-shaped flowers, *Throatwort* or Figwort from the nodules on its rhizome indicating its value against swollen glands and the itch and pain of piles. Neck glands were mostly tuberculous if swollen for long: so, from scrofula came its generic name Scrophularia. It puts out an unpleasant smell which brings pollinating wasps to its shallow well of nectar.

Crimson Shoe

Comfrey for the spitting and pissing of blood [C], mastitis or the gout ... perhaps its most famous application, after Gerard, was as a drink "against the paine in the backe gotten by overmuch use of women". Then, *Bone-Set;* for its roots could be turned into a caking splint - the roots dug up in spring were grated and once packed around a broken limb hardened to the consistency of plaster of Paris. Like Burdock, a wild food - leaves deep-fried in batter.

Comfrey

Meadow Vetchling

Figwort

In poorer times Charlock was generally regarded as a choking weed, and in the Hebrides, where crops are hard to grow, was sold like a vegetable. Another reason it is disliked by farmers is that it harbours the organism responsible for "finger-and-toe" disease of turnips. Although rough and hairy

Charlock

it has pleasing lyre-shaped leaves and rather dainty sepals. Its buried seed can remain dormant, but vital, for decades, and old pasture ploughed for the first time in a generation can explode in yellow just as the battlefields of World War I were turned to red - "a follower of the plough". While it is *farmer's sorrow* it is beekeepers' joy - but like the honey got from oilseed rape it granulates rapidly causing problems with its harvest. However, it can be useful for mixing with liquid honeys such as bramble, if set honey is required. Problems, too, in the use of Watercress - though plentiful in the drainage ditches of the Cuckmere Valley it may be contaminated by eggs of liver fluke discharged by cattle. A raft of pretty flowers floats where the cows come to drink in spring. This is a shallow pond that will dessicate and turn later to a muddy cake. Like an iceberg, most of the Common

Common Water-crowfoot

Water-crowfoot is submerged. Its surface leaves are lobed, those below are feathery and tasselated.

On the very cliff edge grows a plant confined to the southern chalk and very local too. Seen only in short turf and often in association with ancient earthworks, the Field Fleawort may have been transported by the Romans, hence its association with forts and settlements. This specimen is surrounded by little flakes of chalk which have been carried over the cliff in recent gales. It is hung about with a sort of gossamer which I assume affords it some protection from the elements.

Rough Chervil and Bittersweet are both ornamental in the hedgebank. Several features mark this Chervil out and lend it a particular charm - purple spotted stems, fusiform swellings of the stem where the leaf-stalks join, and flower stalks of differing lengths, so its white umbels are not evenly domed. First Cow Parsley, then *cow-mumble,* then Hedge Parsley knit their white lace among the brambles and tall grasses. Bittersweet berries will make you vomit and Rough Chervil will make you spin.

When Tutankhamun's tomb was opened "with

Field Fleawort

the dust of three thousand years" still upon its treasures, flower wreaths and bouquets still lay where they had been "cast on the King's coffin". There were Cornflowers - which no longer grow in Egypt - Water-lilies, Wild Celery and the berries of Bittersweet. And so we know the young King died and was entombed in mid-March or in April.

..... and ever the Yaffle

Rough Chervil

Cow Parsley

Bittersweet

June

Flower-filled, the track is calling, its herbs are happy to be walked on - you cannot harm them - they have been here since the glaciers melted.

As June follows May, the Elder follows Hawthorn giving off its heady scent, as fine as clover and as fine as thyme. Ironically, its wood and leaf both stink: the stink of death, as legend and superstition have it. It was a tree of death, a tree on which criminals were crucified. From their festering corpses this death tree sprang. It became *God's stinking tree* when his Son was nailed to an Elder cross. Judas then hanged himself on an Elder, hence also known as *Judas tree.* Criminality, execution, betrayal and death - beware the Elder. A part of this superstition must have arisen from the poor quality of its wood. To the superstitious it was unwise to make a cradle from the Elder: your bairn would be snatched by goblins. And to burn it would be an invitation to the devil to perch upon your chimney pot, or, worse still, appear from down your chimney. On a lighter note, its pith was used for carving toy figures. In its first year of growth the pith is too sappy, and after the second year of growth the pith shrinks and becomes unusable, but in the second season it is roughly half an inch in diameter and an ideal

Elder

texture for carving. It would be cut into one and a half inch lengths, formed into a human shape, then mounted on a brass round-headed nail to swivel and to rock for a child's amusement.

Less common and more sinister plants yet grow hereabouts: Henbane - the choice of Dr Crippen. Plants poisonous to cattle and horses such as Black Bryony and Ragwort are commonplace, but alkaloid-containing plants toxic to humans also thrive in Downland. The alkaloids impart a warning bitter taste, and the hallucinogenic effects likely deter plant-eating animals. A fifth of all flowering plants contain some alkaloid and their effects on humans range from alerting, as with caffeine, to fatal paralysis, as with the coniine alkaloids of Hemlock. Dry weather and nightfall increase plants' synthetic activity so alkaloid concentrations have a diurnal as well as a seasonal variation.

Perhaps Henbane has a sinister appearance: hunched, its jagged leaves like bats wings, purple veining on the petals. The most extensive colony locally is on the cliff edge growing from friable soil dug out by rabbits. There, it grows with Burdock, Slender Thistle, Yellow Horned Poppy and Buck's-horn Plantain. Gerard knew that it was a narcotic analgesic - "it causeth drowsiness and mitigateth all kinde of pain".

Henbane

He found it growing on dunghills, not on cliff-tops. No plant has a clearer signature: a branch of Henbane in seed is a jawbone with its molars, and it was consequently "boiled with vinegar and holden hot in the mouth" for the toothache. Culpeper boiled the leaves in wine and applied to "swellings all manner: in the scrotum and women's breasts". It is salutary to consider how the apothecaries dealt not just with transient fevers and self-limiting aches and pains - they had to deal with fungating tumours, deep infected wounds and non-viable tissue as in burns and gangrene. The "oil of the seed" was used for tinnitus and "worms in the ears". As an oral treatment Gerard knew of its risks - "the leaves, seed and juice taken inwardly cause an unquiet

Yellow Horned Poppy

Slender Thistle

sleepe, like unto the sleepe of drunkennesse which continueth long and is deadly to the party". Nonetheless, Tudor and Jacobean medical men found it easier to handle than Deadly Nightshade, so it found its niche and was more widely used. Henbane contains hyoscine which is taken for motion sickness, irritable bowel syndrome and as a midriatic in iritis. Long since it was taken by Parkinsonian patients to control their shake. One particularly odd application I chanced upon dates from the 1940s when, as an injection, hyoscine hydrobromide was given to quieten the "death rattle" - those clever doctors, they can treat everything.

Viper's Bugloss, with a stem "speckled like a serpent" and a fruiting head like a snake's was surely intended as an antidote to snake venom, at least according to the "Doctrine of Signatures", whereby the power in a plant is foretold by its form or by its colour. A rough-stemmed plant had to be good for rash or tetters, the shiny seed of Gromwell hardened to be a stone-breaker, any yellow flower a treatment for the jaundice, Samphire, growing on rocks, good against the gravel of the kidney, Yellow Horned Poppies' haemorrhaging sap a treatment for bleeding fluxes. These beliefs were widely held even at a time when scientific method was well developed - but plants have always been invested with magic for better or for worse. In Celtic folklore plants were rained from heaven for the fairies to work good magic: the herbs were seen as a gift for good.

Viper's Bugloss

Adders slip and slide below the rippling grasses on the cliff edge. More usually one sees them sunbathing on chalky tracks in early spring, having just come out of hibernation: one such track in Friston Wood is called Snake Hill. Viper's Bugloss is ubiquitous in Downland: it will grow on cliff-tops,

shingle and is as common in the short grazed turf as in the scrub margin. The flowers are borne on a bristly spike: pink in bud, red-rose on opening and then to blue. Aspish tongues, pink and curvy, flick from the flower's mouth. An extensive colony will put a blue haze on a distant downland slope. Its freely-flowing nectar makes it a magnet for the honeybee. After walking in the heat how pleasant to rest among it and relax to the hypnotic buzz of bees.

In early summer its companions are Slender Thistle and the Wild Mignonette, later clovers and trefoils. Winter sees herds of cows churn up the pasture around their feeding stations. Forlorn when skies are low and grey, and the Sloe is bare and black, these muddy places transform into the most glorious wild gardens by mid-summer when a profusion of Nodding Thistle, Mignonette, Mayweed and Viper's Bugloss spring from the seeds planted by the hooves of cattle. Farmers call this Bugloss the *blue devil,* wishing it away, but apothecaries valued it not just for snake bite - it was used to treat melancholia and Culpeper recommended it for nursing mothers, "to procure an abundance of milk in women's breasts".

Black Adder

Wild Mignonette

Mid-summer, to an orchid bank - attracted and enveloped by the musky scent come the Burnet Moths, Large Skippers and Common Blues. Here they find a bountiful supply of nectar in the spurs of a hundred bright pink Orchids: their strong pink colour harmonising with the white plants in among them, Hedge Bedstraw and the Oxeye Daisy. Less associated with lime-rich soils than Lady's Bedstraw, Hedge Bedstraw produces a delicate effect, its little flowers bunched into puffy cumuli. The *dunder daisy* was a protector of the barn and farmhouse: hung about them to ward off lightning strikes.

Unlike the Burnt Orchid, which takes poorly to any disturbance of its habitat, the Pyramidal Orchid is opportunistic and quick to colonise a suitable site such as the banks of a newly built road. Plotted on botanical tetrads it marches along the spine of the Downs, unwilling to venture off the chalk - unlike the other frequent orchid of the Downs, the Common Spotted, which runs across the Weald to the very borders of the county. As with the Fragrant Orchid, white forms are occasionally seen. This is a long-flowering orchid, which will dally through the summer with tiny Bastard Toadflax, crepey-yellow Rock-rose, and later with creeping, scented Thyme.

A close turf orchid bank

Think of wild roses and you will think of them scrambling through a hedgerow. Well, not always - here is one which has escaped to open slopes: a pink arc

Burnet Moth

under a mid-summer sky. Rosa canina cured a Roman solider of his rabies, hence its name. Consequently not a dog plant, not a worthless growth - useless to physicke - no *dog's siller,* no *dog's mercury,* no *dog's finkle.* In the hedgerow it is kissed by Bittersweet whose five reflexed petals are characteristic of the Solanaceae, a heady cocktail of species including Deadly Nightshade, Henbane and the Thorn-apple. It has no tendrils but it is an entwiner and a scrambler, which will later hang red droplets in the autumn hedge. Red berries are magic berries, so working horses were garlanded with Bittersweet to keep away the hex. All the parts of *woody nightshade* - stem, leaves and berries - are suffused with solanine: another poisonous alkaloid. "The roots and stalks, on first chewing them, yield a considerable bitterness which is soon followed by an almost honey-like sweetness" [C]. Hieronymus Bosch

An orchid bank

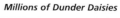

Hedge Bedstraw

Pyramidal Orchid

Millions of Dunder Daisies

Dunder Daisy

Ribwort Plantain

Dog Rose

(16th century) called the plant "Amara dulcis, Dulcis amara, dulcamarum" which William Turner turned to Bittersweet.

The long-spoked stamens of Ribwort Plantain transform a rat's tail to a plant that pleases any jaundiced eye, also a delight to children when they use it for their toy - *a soldier* or a *chimney sweeper*. Minerals lacking in various grasses and legumes are concentrated in this plaintain, hence its presence in the grassland enhances the quality of hay.

Innumerable anthills scar some slopes. Food for the yaffle, also an opportunity for certain creeping species such as Squinancywort and Thyme, which like to ice them with their blossom. A particular and strange relationship has formed between the Yellow Hill Ant and a butterfly, the Chalkhill Blue - the ants mount the caterpillar to take a sweet liquid from it and in return they guard the chrysalis till it hatches one month later. The nursery they build, a makeshift shack, is

Downland anthills

at the base of Horseshoe Vetch, Kidney Vetch or Bird's-foot Trefoil - the caterpillars' fodder. Ants are also attracted to Gorse seeds, more specifically by their brightly coloured caruncles, which hold an oily food-material. Some are dropped by the ants so the Gorse spreads out.

Wild Thyme infiltrates chalk scree, beds into the cliff-top turf, and edges Downland's wending tracks. In summer's heat what could be more pleasant for the traveller than to find respite from the glare of chalk on a scented bed of Thyme. Hot flints, like the mats of blossom, dusted in a fine white powder. Wild Thyme is the commonest of the thymes and is unusually variable: for example there is a smooth as well as a glabrous form. Leaf size, too, is variable. Also on our Downs is the second of Britain's three species, Large Thyme, which has a different scent to that of Wild Thyme: when crushed it smells of petrol. It has hairs on the four angles of its cuboidal stem, not upon its faces,

Chalkhill Blue

whereas Wild Thyme has hairs on opposite sides of its stem. A delicious scent floods out of Thyme when it is trod on. It was recruited for a peculiarly diverse group of illnesses: applied externally for headache - early aromatherapy? - or taken as an infusion for "head-ache, occasioned by the debauch of the preceding night". [c] Good, too, for the spitting of blood and in obstetric practice it helped bring away the afterbirth.

Thymol has been found in its leaves, a compound with antiseptic properties, so perhaps the soothing ointment which was "put on testicles which are swelled" [C] was more than a placebo.

Wild Thyme

Its little friend, Squinancywort, is a "true-blue" chalk-land plant: indeed, almost confined to chalk. A wax-flowered bedstraw which likes to lie among Wild Thyme, its funnel-shaped flowers hanging in cheerful little clusters, pale and beautiful by the stronger pink of Thyme. It was a gargle for the quinsy: squinancy being the quinsy or sore throat. It was a throat plant associated with Judas who was hung by the neck.

Squinancywort

The Hop is native to the woods of Southern England, but not in the thickets and hedgerows hereabout. Hop growing was established on a field basis circa 1550, and its use in commercial brewing was developed from then despite a hiatus when, first, Henry VIIth and then Henry VIIIth proscribed its use in brewing: it was thought to spoil the taste of beer and endanger people's lives. As well as flavouring beer, the hop also clarifies and preserves. Before hops the "wort" derived from the malt was often flavoured, or given bitterness, by plants like Yarrow or Ground Ivy - *alehoof*. Wood sage, which runs freely over our heaths and cliffs, with its hop-like taste and smell, was also used as a bitter. It had clarifying and darkening properties, too. It is unfairly disparaged for its looks. Its flowers are an unusual pale, creamy green and its crinkly sage-like leaves are a fine deep green. The flower has no upper lip and has an unusual five-lobed lower lip beyond which shapely stamens curve. To Wood Sage soil pH is irrelevant, but like the calcicoles amongst which it grows, it takes to well-drained ground. Obviously tough, it flourishes even on bare chalk lashed by dessicating sea spray. Known, too, as *hind-heal*, for a wounded deer would know to seek it out.

Ground Ivy

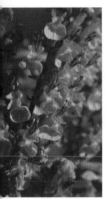

Wood Sage

Culpeper saw how the flowers turned themselves "all one way when they blow". He recommended it as "a sure remedy for the palsy". Oddly, stroke is mentioned only infrequently in medico-botanical books of the 17th century, but would have been prevalent as high blood pressure and diabetes, its main causes, went untreated. The "falling sickness", epilepsy, was far more widely noted and there are many more suggested remedies for that condition.

The ancient botanical works which had greatest impact were practical aids to the use of plants. The standard work for a millennium was De Materia Medica by Dioscorides, a first century Greek who served with the armies of Nero. Subsequent illuminated herbals were full of charm and magic and drew heavily on Dioscorides. In the 16th century the many plants which had not been "authenticated" by him had no Latin name and were therefore named the "naked orphans" or herbae nudae. The earliest surviving copy of De Materia was produced circa AD512, some four centuries after Dioscorides' death. By the late 16th century the holder of the botanical chair at the University of Bologna was still described as "Reader of Dioscorides". The apothecaries of mediaeval England went about the marshes of the Thames and the towns of Kent trying to match the descriptions of plants catalogued on the Mediterranean shores - it was said that Dioscorides "ceased to be a teacher and became a text". As the centuries

Wood Sage

advanced the copyists moved still further from nature and, as a consequence, Dioscorides' effect on botany was then as corrosive as was Galen's effect on medicine. He did, however, regard plants from a physician's point of view or, at least, as a potential pharmacologist. More and more plant-derived chemicals fulfil his prophecy. The herbals and bestiaries of the 16th century involved enormous labour and some are works of incredible beauty. Leonhard Fuchs (1501-1566), a Professor of Medicine - of Fuchsia fame - was instrumental in the cataloguing and accurate illustration of four hundred native German plants and one hundred foreign plants showing the root stocks, flowers, seeds and fruit of each species. He organised teams of artists, one of whom would draw the plant from nature, another who would copy the drawing onto wood blocks and a third would carve the blocks. This return to the reality of nature and the ability to see it with enquiring eyes was slow in coming. Herbs were no longer the flesh of the Gods - their demystification was beginning. Medicine and botany had long been conjoined and it was Paracelsus, one of the fathers of modern medicine, who prophesied their separation. As an example of

Marjoram

this, mercury, an inorganic remedy, became a treatment for syphilis.

Marjoram's flowers hide behind its purplish leafy bracts, and in pink and purple it sits well on sundrenched chalk. On dusty cattle-tramped paths you will see it with the Rock-rose and, where chalk rubble meets shingle, with the Samphire. In times of Plague face cones stuffed with the perfumed branches of Marjoram and Thyme were worn for hygiene. Sweet smelling

A Samphire shore

and nectar rich - from its clumps comes the hum of busy insects. As a pot herb, Origanum onites is superior but Wild Marjoram is still usable. Easy to see why the Romans have this showy plant of hot dry hillsides as a symbol of happiness. The generic name Origanum comes from the Greek "mountain joy". Useful,

Samphire and Marjoram

too: its juice was used as a furniture treatment, imparting a fine fragrance to the wood or "mixed with a little milke, being poured into the eares" took the edge off earache [C]. As well as a restorative for tables, chairs and ears, it was used

Yellow Horned Poppy

Bank of Horned Poppies

Buck's-horn Plantain

to restore an absent appetite [C]. At Cow Gap the shore is lined by great banks of Samphire, one of the few stretches of shore accessible by footpath from the cliff above - it is a delightful place in summer when gay with flowers. For over 300 years May was the time to harvest Samphire, an important wild crop to local economies. It was a brave man who gathered it from the sheer chalk walls of the Isle of Wight, but Samphire, and gulls' eggs, too, were worth the risk. Its fleshy leaves had "a spicy taste with a certain saltnesse" and were keenly sought - it was transported to the London markets in barrels of sea water and sold to be cooked like asparagus or pickled in vinegar. Large quantities of it were shipped out of the Isle of Man where, in past times, it was a significant source of income. Its fat leaves are an adaptation against its harsh environment, just like those of the Wall Pepper 500 feet above.

Strange how a coastal plant should evolve such flimsy petals as the Yellow Horned Poppy's. It skirts our coasts and, sparing the north of Scotland, reaches northwards to the coast of Norway. Snap its stem, root or leaf and it bleeds an acrid yellow juice. Inevitably, with this signature its powdered root was given for the bloody fluxes and other haemorrhages, too: but not without risk as it can induce hallucinations and delusory perceptions. A 'bloody flux' would have been most commonly infective from Shigella or due to inflammatory colitis - certainly a bad enough problem without the complication of hallucinosis. Here on the cliff edge dusty-looking Buck's-horn Plantain cheats the wind, but kept in miniature, flat to the ground, each plant a grey-green stud in a crochet made of hundreds. But on the mild and damp St Agnes, its head the size of a Dandelion plant, its horns are up. The grazing is peppered with the purple *sicklewort* whose flowers blow all summer long. Its muzzle has a hook-shaped upper lip. Before the era of mechanisation, there must have been many accidents involving billhooks, sickles and scythes in the farming year and this was the plant to heal those wounds.

Sicklewort

Otherwise known as *carpenter's heal, wound heal* and *hook heal,* it was as highly esteemed as Bugle for a wound herb.

White form **Spiny Restharrow**

In summer's heat the cliff-top breeze wafts a tarry smell - quite unexpected, this gust of melting asphalt rising from the sward. Restharrow, in mats or bushes, must have creosote running through its sap. Larrea tridentata, the Creosote Bush of the Sonoran Desert, gives off a similar smell. The Apaches made it into poultices. Restharrow is salt-tolerant and flourishes at the base of Beachy Head. In Eastbourne it grows out of gaps in kerbstones. Anathema to farmers, it either tainted milk, made it 'cammocky' (from *cammock* - its Sussex name), or brought the ox-drawn plough or harrow to a halt - another name is *ox-stop.* Its long roots could be so hefty as to be indivisible by a ploughshare. In Greece it is said to be the favourite food of donkeys, to children it was a chewable "liquorice" root. It lacks nectaries so insects attracted by its colours and its scents fly off with no sugary reward.

In times past the paired roots of the Bee Orchid excited more interest than its gorgeous flowers. Of the pair "one waxeth full, the other groweth lank" (C). The filled-out tuber was a provoker of

Common Restharrow

Bee Orchid

Var.chlorantha

lust, the dry and withered one restrained it. As with Autumn Lady's-tresses, a fresh leaf rosette forms before the start of winter. A fox-stone growing in close turf or in open knee-high grass, the Bee is a relatively infrequent orchid though it ranges over Downland: on sheep-trampled terracettes, by old quarry pits, to a stone's throw from the cliffs' sheer drop. When you find it you will sit by it for a while. Gerard posted the first recording from Kent's "barren chalky hills", calling it the bee satyrion with "floures resembling in shape the dead carcasse of a bee". He was aware that various orchids put out flowers in the shape of sundry sorts of living creatures; "flys, honey bees, some like butterflies and other like wasps that be dead". The paradox in the mimicry of the Bee Orchid is that it is more usually self-pollinated and has no use for bees: here it is beyond the northern range of its main pollinator. As the caudicles dry the pollinia are pulled out and drop down upon the stigma. Several varieties can be found locally - this one in washed-out browns and yellows.

Rock-rose has no scent and, like Restharrow, secretes no nectar. In darkness and wet weather its flimsy petals close; this helps self-pollination as the stamens are pushed against the style. However, when open on bright days insects visit it for pollen. It is from pollen that honeybees make brood food to feed their larvae. Where rutty tracks pass among the broad hills Rock-rose follows: it loves the glare of chalk and basks happily in the greatest heat that summer brings. These snaking paths are routes to freedom, to places of wildness and to solitude. Barclay Willis described the sense of release he experienced when on the Downs. Carry no watch, no map...just be there. He did, however, recommend a hairpin on any Downland foray: he once found a linnet caught by the foot in some sheep's wool woven into its nest, which, using his pin, he successfully released.

In amongst the Brambles, the Elders and the Burdocks shoots a sinister chocolate bell: *dwale* or Deadly Nightshade. Someone once wrote that its berries "attracted the unwary like a beautiful woman". Its black berries ooze a purple juice which seems bland to hover wasps, but if taken in quantity by a human, delirium comes first, then death. A safer way to administer belladonna is to put the leaves on your temples [G] - "sleepe will come -

Rock-rose

especially if moistened by wine vinegar". Its alkaloids include atropine, solanine and hyoscyamine. Atropine can be used as a cardiac accelerator after a heart attack or in other situations where the heart runs dangerously slow. Nightshade seeds frequently turn up in the excavations of Roman house refuse which suggests it may have been quite commonly cultivated for domestic use. Having

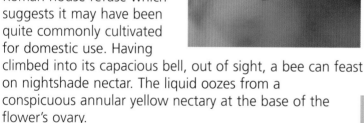

Deadly Nightshade

climbed into its capacious bell, out of sight, a bee can feast on nightshade nectar. The liquid oozes from a conspicuous annular yellow nectary at the base of the flower's ovary.

White Bryony

With the passing of the summer *tetterberries* will redden and proclaim White Bryony, a common Downland plant. But now it is retiring and pale, hardly apparent in the camouflage of the scrub. Vine-like leaves, pretty fine-veined flowers and coiled tendrils are all quite pleasing features. It is a grabber and a twiner, using its "small claspers" [C] to gain support. It is sometimes prone and spreads flat along the ground, like a jellyfish stranded on a beach, if it seeds a distance from the scrub. I have seen it scramble over the very cliff edge, dangling fruit above the sea. As the Black Bryony has a black tuber, White

White Bryony

Lizard Orchid

Bryony has a white one. This is our only native species of the Cucumber family and a poisonous one, too. Of some ninety families of plants, over thirty are represented by a single genus, eg, Frankeniaceae and the Cucurbitaceae. This highlights the impoverishment of our flora consequent upon the Ice Age - any of these families with a single genus in our flora have multiple genera beyond our shores. Like the cucumber it was cultivated at one time. There had been an important trade in Bryony tubers which were used as an ersatz mandrake, an expensive Mediterranean import valued for its medicinal qualities, particularly in relation to fertility and birth. In the case of childlessness it would take magic to the womb. When taken by mouth great care was needed in dosing as it could induce violent vomiting - it was also known as *death warrant*. As a pessary it was used at stillbirth to "draw forth the dead child" [C]. Mandrake root grew in the shape of a man and, according to legend, only under gallows - given to the crucified to ease their pain. There were risks to pulling a mandrake root: pulled by a man the plant would give a great shriek, so violent as to kill him. It was best, therefore, to tie a dog to the plant and have it draw the root. Bryony's white root can be very large and heavy. Gerard had seen a Bryony root that "waied halfe an hundred weight and of the bignesse of a child of a yeere old". The root would be carved into the form of a child by country tramps and sold on. Bryony mandrakes could be given hair by sewing the head with grass seed. Culpeper cautioned that such were the dangers of Bryony that only a skilled apothecary should handle it. Otherwise it was given for a ragbag of disorders including ringworm - hence its name *tetterberry* - and its leaves were put on "filthy sores" and gangrenous extremities as a cleanser. A drug which confers maximum risk and minimum benefit. Like Beech and Cowslip it is a calciphile.

No trace of the Lizard Orchid for some eighty years in the Downs around East Dean, but now it is back. Each flower a wild extravagance, be it a trailing lizard's tail or a chameleon's shooting tongue.

Hop Trefoil, usually small-headed like Black Medick, occasionally appears in a larger form - this may relate to its earlier cultivation as a fodder crop. It is one of the most prolific of the turf flowers in June and July. Later its bright yellow heads turn to paper brown. This is what the Irish call the shamrock, a good luck plant.

Hop Trefoil

Among the cliff-top trefoils and clovers creeps cheerful Cinquefoil. It likes a grassy knoll and often, like the Small-flowered Buttercup, adorns the entrance to a rabbit hole. Its petals lack the beauty of the Rock-rose but its runners are a jolly red. Like its relatives in the Rose family, Tormentil and Silverweed, it is a healer. Gerard had it "cinkefoile", and in Sussex it is *five fingers*, the

Small-flowered Buttercup

Cinquefoil

Biting Stonecrop

Pentaphyllon. It was known to the Mediterraneans and given as an anti-malarial. Here it was made into a witches ointment to which Bacon (1627) alluded: made of "the fat of children digged out of their graves". More prosaically a decoction of the root assuaged the toothache.

By the precipice, the surging sea below, Biting Stonecrop flowers unconcerned. By its yellow there is a flash of black - a glint of chalk is in the Jackdaw's blue-grey eye. It nestles in the Buck's-horn Plantain and by the Small Hare's-ear, its fleshy flowering stem erect; so it was *trique madam*, anglicised by Gerard to *prick-madam*, naturally, an aphrodisiac. *Welcome-home-husband-how-ever-drunk-you-be* must be one of the oddest monikers in plant vernacular. Most thunder

Eyebright

Small
Hare's-ear

plants activate a storm but here is a plant that wards off thunder, but only if you plant it on your roof. John Evelyn, c.1688, had it as a plant for the kitchen garden along with Samphire, Alexanders and Wood Sorrel. Its leaves are plump and peppery, a fine addition to a salad of crisp leaves. Culpeper bruised Stonecrop leaf and found it "excellent in paralytic contractions of the limbs", a consequence of stroke and other neurological disorders: more likely the recovery was spontaneous. The Small Hare's-ear is a very rare plant - confined in England to the Beachy Head area, Berry Head, S Devon and the Channel Isles. Slender Hare's-ear is also scarce in Britain but is seen on a number of West Sussex sites.

Another parasitic plant is the widespread herb, Eyebright. Low lying, ideally adapted to cliff living, more than 25 different species of Euphrasia are scattered across the wildest cliffs in Britain. Some species are extremely local, eg, E.Rhumica, confined to the tiny Inner Hebridean island of Rhum. The larger flowered species are pollinated by bees and hover flies while the smaller ones tend to be self-pollinated. Euphrasia nemerosa, the most widespread of the genus, feeds off roots of clovers and of plantains. Its detailed flower markings, in purple and yellow, recall ceramic art. Its juice, an ancient eye drop.

Knotted Hedge-parsley

Nearer the cliff edge, where Scabious and Knapweed heads sit tightly on the turf, grow other plants in miniature. Though conditions so

Rampion Bank

reduce the cliff-top plants, their flower size is maintained. Knotted Hedge-parsley in a favourable environment will reach 35 cm, here but 5 cm. "Knotted" from the crowding of its fruits, queer half-bald things with bristles only on one side. Round-headed Rampion, the "Pride of Sussex", growing from the driest rock, has an inky crown befitting the King of Downland. First found on Silbury in 1634 by a party of apothecaries on their way to Bath, and only on the chalk: from Dorset through to Kent, though mostly it is a South Downs plant. Drop down from a Downland top by way of a sunken

track and there, on the bostal banks, you will see it waving in the short tan grasses. On its spoke-like tufts will be the Six-spot Burnet Moth. These ancient tracks coming off the northern shoulder of the Downs are stuck with black and glassy flints. Here the turf is ancient and herb-rich, capping rows of barrows, burial sites from Neolithic times. The Saxons when they came to Downland kept off the tops: to them they were giant graveyards, where alarming spirits roamed, where now the Small Copper flits. From here, look north across the Weald - Spiked Rampions' sole repository.

Six-spot Burnet Moth

Eye-catching Sainfoin may be a Downland native, and I like to think it is. Nowadays it is cultivated less for sheep and cattle fodder - here it runs free amongst the Crow Garlic, Sea Radish and Alexanders of the cliff. Its exuberant coxcombs turned and jostled by the afternoon's stiffening sea breeze.

Sea Radish is usually a coastal plant of the west, rather than the east, of Britain but around Cow Gap it flourishes. A crowd of simple yellow flowers, impressive against the summer sky. Each fruit contains two, no more than three, seeds designed to bob and shift with the tide till they find landfall. Its leaves are

Spiked Rampion

Sainfoin

Sea Radish

Round-headed Rampion

Crow Garlic

Fragrant Orchid

large and rather grand with lots of overlapping leaflets.

Some species occupy a large variety of habitats which at first sight seem quite incompatible - the Fragrant Orchid is one such plant. Further north it has its feet in fenny spots but here it lives on well-drained grassy hills. It is home to the Common Crab Spider, which cleverly changes colour to match the flowers among which it lurks. It is after the Six-spot Burnet Moth, the Large Skippers and various long-tongued moths which pollinate the orchid. The Downland form smells of orange blossom, the marsh-living one, I hear, of cloves. As with Selfheal and Viper's Bugloss white forms are occasionally cast up: a particularly lovely form. Flower colour comes from pigments contained in plastids, intracellular structures, or from anthocyanins dissolved in cell-sap. The former gives us shades of yellow, the latter reds, blues and purples. Hybridisation between the Fragrant Orchid and other orchid species does occur, but only the hybrid of the Common Spotted Orchid is found in Sussex. Of three sub-species, two are found between Eastbourne and Lewes.

A leek fit only for crows. Like Restharrow, Crow Garlic tainted the milk of grazing animals - farmers even feared that a cow inhaling its vapours would yield milk likely to be spoiled. At Whitbread Hollow it looks quite bohemian clustered by the Radish: the points of the purple bulbils wispy and criss-crossing in a beautiful green tangle.

Disdained by rabbits, Hound's-tongue grows freely about their warrens - perhaps it is the ratty smell of the plant that puts them off. Gerard thought it smelt of dog's urine. Soft and hairy, its leaves tongue-shaped, its flowering stems curling at their tips: a host of signatures here. Being hairy it was a cure for baldness. Culpeper, who had a fine head of hair, in fact he had what would nowadays be called a "mullet", was sensitive and called baldness "the falling away of the hair". Boil the juice of its leaves in hog's lard and slap it on then wait... and wait... From its scorpioid inflorescence hang little bell-shaped flowers of a unique red-brown hue - called elsewhere "a sordid red". The shape and texture of the leaf is like a hound's tongue. Have the leaf in your shoe

Crow Garlic

and it will "tie the tongues of hounds". Specifically, to keep them from barking at you, have it under your big toe. Painful piles? - bake the root wrapped in wet papers "under the embers" and apply as an assuaging suppository. Often a plant of waste places but most handsome in the shingle. Further north, be it North Wales, Scotland or Ireland, it is almost always by the sea. Dull compared to its cousin, Blue Hound's-tongue, a plant of abandoned olive groves.

Hound's-tongue

The paleness of its petals and the wavy edges of its leaves make Mignonette so pleasing. This *little darling* is much smaller than its relative the Weld. It can

Blue Hound's-tongue

aspire to be a metre tall and often grows in clumps, a pale yellow mist hanging on the slopes. It likes the cliff edge, too. Some colonies are quite extensive and will flower continually past summer to the very end of autumn. The pallor of its stems and heads contrasts nicely with the darkness of its glossy leaf, all puckered about its margins, like a green seaweed that has been blown inland.

Southern English calcicoles, Bastard Toadflax and Musk Orchid both. This tiny stellate 'toadflax' grows from thin, dry soils in short, tough turf where Kidney Vetch and Thyme keep company. It steals from the roots of the other herbs and grasses. Early in his search for British species, in 1903 Keble Martin (illustrator of The Concise British Flora) spent a

Bastard Toadflax

Musk Orchid

Man Orchid

summer holiday on the western end of the Downs at Winchester. There he drew Kidney Vetch, Bastard Toadflax and the Frog Orchid. I can imagine his excitement at finding the little Thesium. Small, too, Musk Orchid, thumb high, at Malling Down, the eastern limit of its Sussex range. In these poorest of soils with its shallow roots it is susceptible to drought to a point where it may fail to flower after a prolonged dry summer. In the 1960s many thousands could be counted in a good year, now they may be counted on a hand.

The Man Orchid used to grow at Alciston and at the Crumbles. The former site was destroyed in 1969 by modern farming methods and the latter when a marina was built just east of Eastbourne. It reappeared, however, in Offham near Lewes in 1997 near a site first documented in 1863. Currently the important Sussex colony is further west, near Pyecombe on the western side of Brighton. Its name derives from its labellum configured like a hanging man.

I have, once only, chanced upon the Star-of-Bethlehem though it is likely a native of the southern woods and grasslands. Turner wished to call it *dogges onion* from its German name but Gerard's Star-of-Bethlehem rightly won through. Striped green and white, it is a garden favourite. The larger O.umbellatum has, too, escaped the garden and may be naturalised. Whether growing wild or dried in hay, the plant is poisonous to cattle. Strange, then, that pilgrims on their way to Mecca took dried bulbs to eat along their way. Also a clock flower, *nap-at-noon* shuts early in the day and is very responsive to the appearance and disappearance of the sun. More pale bells, these streaked in green and hanging off a triangular stem, found serendipitously in a Blackthorn thicket - Triquetrous Garlic. It naturalised very successfully in the South West and is rampant in the Scillies, where it invades the bulb fields and is a headache to commercial growers.

Triquetrous Garlic

Star-of-Bethlehem

Only three kinds of English thistle were recorded before Gerard. He added the Nodding Thistle to the catalogue, naming it the *musk thistle* from its scent. 'Nodding' is more apposite: the drooping of its head lends particular charm. The head is backed by an array of spiky bracts and just below the down-turned flower, the stem has lost its prickles, instead it is smooth and downy, like an Achilles heel. It flowers in the places filled with Mignonette and with it will bloom at Christmas. It benefits from

disturbance and will build strong colonies in pasture and in field corners where cows have churned the soil. W. H. Hudson once encountered a young shepherd on the Downs: "He had loose-fitting grey clothes on and a round grey peakless cap: and for ornament he had fastened in the middle of it, where there had perhaps once been a top-knot or ball, a big woolly thistle flower. I was really very curious to note how that one big thorny flower-head with its purple disc harmonised

Nodding Thistle

with everything about the boy and gave him a strange distinction."

Pale blue flecks of Flax in a bright yellow sea of Cat's-ear waving in the summer's breeze. Both plants of short grassland near the sea, wonderful to lie among, looking through them skywards. Like others of the Compositae, the Cat's-ear is impressive in profusion. Flax is grown commercially for linseed in these parts and a Downland top painted in its powder blue is an arresting sight. It has been a source of fibre for linen and linseed oil for more than 7000 years - linen made by soaking the flax stems in water then beating and separating the fibres. A related species was used in the wrappings of Egyptian mummies. In the wild it is now either a relic of cultivation or a recent escape.

Flax

Cat's-ear

Wall Butterfly

Wild Clary

Red Star Thistle

Fiddle Dock

The pale Flax drops its blossom in the afternoon, sad that it is so short-lived, but new flowers will appear and it will put out its lovely little bells through all of summer. Cat's-ear roots are relished by the pig. Up its stem spiral the little 'cat's ear's', tiny burnt-looking, scale-like bracts. Two other Cat's-ear species, the Common Spotted and the Smooth, grow in the United Kingdom but they are far less prevalent.

Where the sharply sloping chalk drops from High and Over to the river, scrub gives way to grass. Here Star Thistle, Wild Clary and the Fiddle Dock grow happily together. The Wall bask on tracks that skirt the scrub. First sclarea, which became clarie, corrupted to clear-eye then to Clary. Its seed when moistened swells and exudes a slimy mucilage and this was used to clear debris from the surface of the eye: "put a seed in the eye and let it remain till it drops out of itself" [C]. Culpeper thought it blasphemous that it was called *Christ's eye* because it "cured diseases of the eyes", but he goes on to recommend it as an "admirable help to provoke lust". By the Clary are extensive banks of Red Star Thistle. A very rare thistle, this thistle, and Frog Firle is one of its few sites. It forms little hedges a metre high which can stretch for twenty metres. It seeds on the raised track that runs along the Cuckmere river where it is trampled on by cattle and by equally unknowing walkers. Looking, too, as if it has been trampled, the Fiddle Dock has a squashed-down look about it. The fiddle in the dock is from its leaf.

Like the Burdock, Goat's-beard has a long tap root and was previously a shepherd's vegetable - some preferred it to the carrot. Among the handsomest of Downland's plants, whether in flower or in seed, it is elegant of stem, bud and leaf, its spare, attenuated petals surrounded by a circle of tapered bracts. Not just the shepherd's lunch also the shepherd's clock: a flower that closes up at noon. Many are its clock names: *Jack-go-to-bed-at-noon, nap-at-noon, etc.* One of the most uplifting sights on the chalky slopes is its golden clock. A blowball, as spectacular and precise in its arrangements as the fan vaulting in a great cathedral. White Salsify, a sweet edible root, comes from a Mediterranean relative.

Descending a grassy track, having kept to the ridges that link the hill tops, in my mind's eye I was already settled, a beer in hand, in the cool and dimness of the village pub below. Lower down I passed a place of Sow Thistles and runty Hawthorns. Here and there a fleck of Madder - nothing that would caress the eye. But in the short grasses bordering a barley field peeps an unexpected bloom - a Corncockle, then another. Systematically eradicated from the cornfield, it was loathed for adulterating flour: consequently it is now a rarity. Long sepals extending beyond the petals, and its inner veining mark it out and give it the stamp of beauty. Its seeds were originally

Goat's-beard

brought in from the Mediterranean as a contaminant of crop seeds. How it grows here, far from any gardens is a mystery. It has been known to grow near turkey farms, arriving in the seed they fatten on: perhaps it fell from the turn-ups of a turkey farmer.

Goat's-beard blowball

A "blood-root" drawn from the machair by Hebridean fisherman to tan their nets. As white Meadowsweet gives a black dye, yellow Tormentil yields a red one. It has a long flowering season and is tolerant of many different soils. It is widespread on the cliff-edge turf: in early summer with Milkworts and Salad Burnet then with Dropworts and Burnet Rose. It is plentiful in the acid topsoil of Lullington Heath where it grows amongst the heathers, closing its petals when it is dark and wet. It sits, too, content in the spongy bogs of distant Sutherland with sticky Sundew and the Butterwort, a world away from the porous chalk of Downland.

Tormentilla means torture in mediaeval Latin and tormina in Latin

White Salsify

Corncockle

Tormentil

means a colic: so the plant of the torment of colic. Gerard thought it beneficial in cases of diarrhoea, particularly if the powdered root was given "in the water of a smithy's forge". Forge water, when I was a boy, was a Highland cure for warts. Culpeper put it to various uses: some bizarre - to sit in a bath of tormentil-infused water was "a remedy against abortion". The root could also be plugged into a dental cavity to dull the toothache.

Tiny points of colour catch the eye of the silent traveller - Scarlet Pimpernel and Basil Thyme, two low-slung creepers of crumbling banks and tracks that are rarely walked upon. The first is frequent and ubiquitous, the second is rather a scarce and local plant. Sheep are fond of Basil Thyme and it is said that it flavours mutton. The sheep cropping the short herbage inevitably consume large numbers of the white snails (zoned snails), which appear through autumn in fantastic numbers - said by some Downland shepherds in the past also to impart a distinctive flavour to South Downs lamb. Generations of farmers with their grazing animals helped keep back the scrub and the grasses short. This,

Scarlet Pimpernel

Basil Thyme

with the poor quality of Downland soil, encouraged a richness of turf herbs. Sheep movements on the Downs in days past were on a grand scale. Bostals were paths used to funnel sheep from the brows to the bottoms. In May, after lambing, the ewes were let onto the Downs after being folded through the winter. At lambing time the "little valerian", Lamb's-lettuce, first appears. The lambs were still crib-fed on cut vetches and winter oats, and in June were weaned and then put out on Sainfoin ley. Then was the time for the ewes to be washed and sheared. In fine weather shearing was an outdoor job, but if the weather was bad the sheep would be penned in a barn. Inevitably the hand shears could nick the skin and in olden days tar-boys would dab the wounds, sometimes with wood ash, to keep infection out. Mild beer, known as "swanky", was provided for the shearing gangs and it was the tar-boy's duty to fill the shearers' mugs with beer, then after the day's work, with stronger ale.

The Pimpernel, not always scarlet - pink or white or even blue - and sometimes a single stem will carry flowers that are both blue and red. Perceived as a cheerful plant it was used to dispel melancholy. Gerard particularly associated it with harvest time when farm folk used it for a barometer - "behold the floures of pimpernel whereby they know the weather that shall follow the next day after ... if the floures close up it betokeneth raine and foule weather". Also known as *shepherd's sundial* it

Blue Pimpernel

Stunted form

Corn Salad

Centaury

opens between 8 am and 3 pm. But the Downland shepherd had more accurate timekeeping devices: he used to cut a sundial in the turf and might have several of these shadow clocks along his walks. When he came upon one he would insert his crook to get the time.

Centaury speckles slopes - a scatter of hardly discernible points of pink. But here and there it pushes up a posy, a ready-made bouquet of starry blossom, like a little bush. On an exposed cliff-top it can be quite stunted. It has many ecotypes and they can look so different as to cause a confusion in their classification. It is our commonest native gentian and is now smiling, then coy, among the frothy Dropworts and the shrubby Dyer's Greenweed.

Dyer's Greenweed

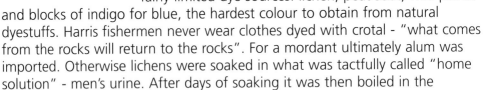

Field Madder

I know the Dyer's Greenweed on a gentle Down where, earlier, the Spider Orchid showed and where, later in the summer, Moon Carrot will glow by night. Some plants transcend their surroundings - Moth Mullein growing from a heap of rusting scrap - but show me a plant that is not bettered by being in its own community of herbs and grasses. It is an attractive, heath-like, creeping plant whose root dye was used in making greens with woad. It was backbreaking work in Napoleonic times pulling the root:- women's work, and 1s and 6d a hundredweight. Take most chalk herbs, boil, and you will get a dye - Nettle and Red Clover give a yellow - the commonest result. In the turf and on the tree bark many lichens extend the dyer's palette. The best known dyeing lichen is crotal, or "rock beard", a coarse rock lichen, its reddish brown the hallmark of Harris tweed. Some of these natural dyes are substantive, requiring no mordant, an additional advantage. The colours in Harris tweed came from fairly limited dye sources: lichen, peat soot, wild plants and blocks of indigo for blue, the hardest colour to obtain from natural dyestuffs. Harris fishermen never wear clothes dyed with crotal - "what comes from the rocks will return to the rocks". For a mordant ultimately alum was imported. Otherwise lichens were soaked in what was tactfully called "home solution" - men's urine. After days of soaking it was then boiled in the

Dropwort

solution. Other mordants could be manufactured simply, for example a lump of iron in a tub of vinegar, and had predictable effects on the colour that was ultimately produced. Dyers' work is skilful if a clear rather than a muddy dye is to be achieved. It is important to know which part of the plant to use. To dye red with Lady's Bedstraw use its root bark and for a black the root, not flower, of Tormentil. Red also in the root of prostrate Madder, but for scarlet R.Tinctorium was pre-eminent. The age of the plant, too, makes a difference to the colour it gives up, for example the colour from old heather is quite different from that of young heather.

All about is gentle Dropwort.

Two plants we are well used to seeing against the turbid turquoise water of the Channel are now in bloom. Both were brought to these shores to grow in gardens, later to escape: Spur Valerian and the Tamarisk. Spur Valerian was introduced as a garden plant in the 16th century and Gerard had it in his London garden. Its seeds parachuted out but took a long time to reach our coast. Indeed it was rare even in nearby Oxfordshire by 1890, not recorded in our shingle till World War II. Its generic name, Centranthus (Gr. flower spur), refers to a tubular projection at the base of each flower. Colourful and vigorous. Unjust, I say, the soubriquet *drunkard's nose*. Best on bare white cliff or rooted in the shingle.

Spur Valerian

For centuries marl, and later lime, were put on the heavy Wealden clay to improve the texture of the soil and to fertilise it. The practice of marling on the Weald resulted in a pit at the corner of virtually every field. Lime first came into extensive use in the 17th century. As the chalk pits of the Downs were inaccessible it was not until improvements in transportation in the 18th century that marl was supplanted. The new turnpikes of the 1780s brought an end to marling. Below the northern scarp vast areas of summer fallow were whitened with lime in readiness for wheat. The scarp itself is pocked with chalk pits, many of which grew into impressive workings. In some pits the chalk was shipped out rather than carted out, for example, chalk was shipped from the pits at Holywell near Eastbourne to the lime kilns in Hastings. 18th century land reclamations on the Downs were also responsible for extensive chalk quarrying. Large pits on the Berwick and Alciston Downs directly relate to those activities. Chalk in its lumpy raw state was applied to acid ground, laid a ton and a half to an acre. Now the pits lie undisturbed, silent, where Wild Strawberries redden and turn oh-so sweet.

Tamarisk

Along Eastbourne's seafront the Tamarisk is handsome against the breaking waves and the seam of sea and sky. It has naturalised along this coast but, still, is mostly seen by habitation. The first English Tamarisk was in the garden of the Bishop of London at Fulham Palace and later

Wild Carrot

Gerard had it in his garden. It can thole the salty blast and bend to the wind. Cornish and Scillonian fishermen used the whippy stems to make their lobster pots. Various superstitions are attached to drinking cups hewn from the wood

of different trees: ivy wood cups for whooping cough, while the magic in a tamarisk cup would dispel melancholia. The Egyptians valued it to treat serious infections such as leprosy, while here Tamarisk bark was sometimes given to rickety children [C].

Wild Carrot sends a great white swell breaking over Downland's slopes and hollows. Move close and you will see, nestling in the very centre of each flower's crown, a single purple floret. Those were individually garnered for the power that was invested in them to stop convulsions. Later in the year its fruiting head looks like a bird's nest balanced on a stick, an effect most apparent when the heads tighten up in wet conditions.

The best of the compositae for show and brightness is the Field Milk-thistle: big floral sunbursts of golden yellow. And for an arresting show in pink, Musk Mallow - sadly quite scarce. A rarity is Hispid Mallow, which is found only in a handful of native sites. Its splendid hairiness best appreciated by viewing it through a magnifying lens.

Field Milk-thistle

Musk Mallow

Impressive in its tallness and the quality of its leaf: big, bright leaves, finely nicked about their edges with a hint of purple veining flowing from the purple in the stems. On the Lizard Angelica stands proud of Heather and the Asphodel. Here it is something of a rarity - amongst the Alder, its feet in clag, where the chalk has dipped below the clay. "Large and beautiful ... it is as good a preservative

Hispid Mallow

as grows" according to Culpeper. He described how stalks, as well as roots, could be candied and how "it does wonderfully help" virtually every medical condition known to

him: "filthy ulcers to colic, gout and sciatica". Nowadays a different species, archangelica, is used commercially.

A mint of wetland, damp hollows, the haunts of damselflies: pretty Skullcap. Its rather sinister sounding name relates to a hump on its calyx. De l'Obel first recorded it in 1576 and called it a loosestrife with a small galerum: a leather skull helmet worn by the Romans. This later suggested the name of Skullcap. Paired flowers marked in blue and white facing in the same direction ensure that it is unmistakable.

Angelica

Gerard's was the first botanical record of Sneezewort, a natural substitute for Pellitory of Spain. Its fiery root was held in the mouth for toothache and a powder made from the plant was "sniffed up the nose" to induce sneezing to "clear the head of slimy humours". [c] Another sneeze plant is Hoary Pepperwort - its seeds were gleaned for a pepper surrogate. An alien from southern Europe it was first recorded in Ramsgate in 1827, now but a nuisance to the farmer.

Sneezewort

Its flowers start the day facing east and end it turned towards the setting sun. Heliotropic Weld is no longer useful, just a wild plant once more with Viper's Bugloss and cousin Mignonette. It can achieve surprising heights - a Downland "saguaro". On Lullington Heath it grows through carpets of bell heather. Once it was a dyer's plant made into bright yellows and also greens - so in Sussex it was *green weed*. Unlike woad it is a native. In neighbouring Kent it was grown commercially. However large quantities were still brought in from France by textile makers over a period of many years.

Hoary Pepperwort

Skullcap

Like the Corncockle, Gromwell, the poor relative of Purple Gromwell, grew in cereal fields. It is not seen often but I know of one massive stand of it near Butts Brow. It grows, too, in the Ling by Belle Tout. Its flowers are drab, care-worn and somewhat insignificant but its fruits are quite unusual. This is the "stone seed" of Dioscorides: bluey-white, well-bossed nutlets known also as *grey millet*. Take a stone to break a stone. Bladder and kidney stones would have been so much more

Gromwell *Holly flower* *Guelder Rose*

Speckled Wood

Fly Orchid

common in the pre-antibiotic era when urinary infections went unchecked and so the apothecaries were not short of treatments to recommend.

Fine-grained wood from Holly, white as the blossom of the Guelder Rose, was useful - it was suited for inlaying and as it was so hard could be stained black to simulate ebony, often for a teapot handle. Only the female Holly bears red berries and only the lower leaves have spines to fend off browsing animals - the upper leaves are spineless. The waxy surface of the leaf minimises water loss - a leaf which can last four years. In pre-Christian times it had a power over evil, a protective magic was held within its sap. And in its red fruits, too. Red was a healing colour. Tramps would seek out the protection of a Holly hedge. When the Holly was embraced by Christian culture it became the blooded crown of thorns - before the Christians took it, it was put against house goblins.

Crowds of Speckled Woods patrol secret glades and clearings where Fly Orchid and Sweet Woodruff dazzle above the litter of the beechwood floor. Fly Orchid is said to grow on the northern slope at Willingdon but I believe that colony has died away. Happily its spikes still open in shady woods by Lewes. Never a common orchid in Sussex but there are numerous sites in the beech hangers of West Sussex and Hampshire where it can be seen with Sword-leaved Helleborine. The "eyes" of the Fly exude the nectar to which male digger wasps are drawn. The orchid also emits a pheromone mimicking the odour of the female wasp which persuades the male to attempt copulation with the flower. No matter how doomed the attempt it works well for the orchid as its pollen masses are worked off. The female wasps reach maturity some days later: then the orchid is forsaken. Galium odoratum, a fragrant Bedstraw - for stuffing and strowing - is, oddly, scentless: only when picked does its delicious scent emerge and left in chests of drawers the dry plant puts out scent, seemingly forever. Beguiling *sweet grass*, alternatively *star grass* from its whorls of shapely leaves edged with minute forward-angled prickles. Successful in diverse habitats: sat in a Sussex glade it is hard to see it in one's mind's eye high on a Scottish mountain.

Beech is the natural climax woodland on the shallow soils that overlie the chalk of Southern England. In mast years, every third or fourth, the tree gives a particularly heavy crop of nuts of which the Nuthatches are particularly fond. Beech woods impose an unfair double handicap on associated plants - keeping poor soils dry and allowing little light. Nonetheless, there are plants which have adapted to these conditions - Yellow Bird's-nest and Bird's-nest Orchid are both pale brown saprophytes, adapted to the dryness and the gloom. They do not require sunlight to manufacture food but obtain it from decaying leaves in which they root. I have yet to find them here.

Strange Spurges have neither petals nor sepals and an odd stalked ovary, hung with crescentic yellow glands. This is a plant of Southern England, of sodden woodland clearings.

Wood Spurge

And in these damp disregarded places is Hogweed. In Ireland it is *the singer:* come the winter, cold blasts make owlish notes from brittle skeletons, but now it puts a rather grand white frill around the barley baize. Like the Guelder, the flowers on the umbel's rim are larger. It deserves a better English name: in Sweden they call it hyperbolically the *herb of heaven.* It was mainly for a pig fodder that it was gathered and lashed in bundles. Yet more unfairly disregarded plants: Rosebay Willowherb and Common Vetch. A pink mirage on a far-off incline - here is a plant that

Sweet Woodruff

can put an imprint on the landscape. Dismissed now as a weed it was well regarded by Gerard as a garden plant, beautiful but too invasive to invite inside your fence. Much, much later with the growth of railways and industrial wasteland it spread and spread. So quickly does it colonise burnt woodland that its other name is *fireweed*. It took hold of urban bomb sites in World War II and its

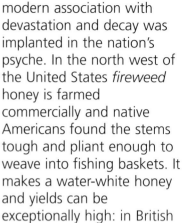

modern association with devastation and decay was implanted in the nation's psyche. In the north west of the United States *fireweed* honey is farmed commercially and native Americans found the stems tough and pliant enough to weave into fishing baskets. It makes a water-white honey and yields can be exceptionally high: in British Columbia 100 lbs per hive is not an uncommon average. Its seeds may germinate even when their capsule is still on the parent plant. Seed vitality is extremely variable between the species: some Willows can only

Hogweed

Common Vetch

Rosebay Willowherb

germinate within one week of shedding. Acorns lose their power of germination in a few months while the seeds of Kidney Vetch lay dormant for ninety years, then fire up.

Prettier than Tufted Vetch, Common Vetch was an introduction as a cattle fodder. Now wild, among the Buttercups and Wild Carrot......

In brackish places Water Dropworts, Sea Plantain and Celery-leaved Buttercups are now in flower. This species of buttercup grows in the water meadows of the Cuckmere where indolent cattle graze and Lapwings risk their eggs. Like its relatives it is very toxic and is probably the commonest cause of Buttercup poisoning. Fortunately it is safe in hay. Sea Plantain stands expectant - it keeps wet with the flux of tides. As the river nears the sea great clumps of Water Dropworts, man-high, spring from the salty marshes. There are many Water Dropworts: Fine-leaved, and Parsley Water

Dropworts are quite common, but loveliest is the Tubular Water Dropwort, seen here growing freely in the salt with Meadow Vetchling. But equally happy in the freshwater drainage ditches of the Pevensey Levels just off Downland's eastern edge.

Ponds are few on this ridge of chalk but on a crest near Jevington there is a fine one where dragonflies dart around the birds that have flown in to slake their thirst. By the Reed Mace the pineapple-like leaves of Water Soldier cradle its fine white flower. An odd find here in Downland for it comes from the Norfolk Broads. The submerged aquatic, happily risen to the surface to float its blossom.

Water Dropwort

Tubular Water Dropwort

Water Soldier

Sea Plantain

..... and ever the Yaffle

A gentle union

Tubular Water Dropwort

Celery-leaved Buttercup - Lapwing eggs

July

A flash of Wheatear's rump and tail before it drops from sight, like a chalk - cased flint tumbliing off the cliff, then suddenly a Peregrine bullet rips the sky while untrammelled Fulmars, half-interested in the traveller, turn their heads and wonder why humans keep to tracks. By such tracks tinkers set up camp, along them fisher-folk carried their catch inland to Downland villages. No commerce now - routes to silent gardens where seed is planted by the wind, to sun-filled coombes.... to Downland's heart. (But migratory birds, I hear you say, keep to highways in the sky).

At Hope Gap there is a most unusual habitat which holds plants of interest throughout the year. A wide skelp of Privet, kept only inches deep, makes a flower-shot "maquis" on the rising slope behind the Gap. The Privet Hawk-moth caterpillar is in heaven - large and green with zigzag stripes along the flanks. Privet, and later Ragwort, is a source of ill-tasting honey. Bees themselves can be poisoned by certain nectars, such as Locoweed in the U.S.A., and nectar garnered from Buckeye blossoms, trees closely related to horse chestnut, poisons the brood rather than the foragers. Nectar from certain late-flowering limes appears inimical to bumblebees, which can be seen dead or dying under flowering Tilia Petiolaris.

Privet

The Violet has long since wilted and the Purple Orchid too - now it is the turn of Iris and the Teasel. The *adder's mouth,* with dark-veined tepals: tongues of

73

grey-blue and purple-livid-slate: queer and fanciful. I would rather have it as the *gladdon* than the Stinking Iris - only stinking when its leaves are crushed to let the smell of raw beef out: the name *roast beef plant* is a misnomer. Some desert plants stink of rotting meat to attract their pollinating insects but an odour trapped inside a leaf seems to serve little function - but all innards stink. From the cliff it found its way into the physic garden - grown to purge.

Pink-stained lace is on the *kex*, half shaded by tall hedges meandering above deep-sunk tracks. "Up North" Upright Hedge-parsley is *red kex*.

A hundred flowers can crowd the spike of a Broad-leaved Helleborine. I know it from the shadows of the beech , half wishing light, cautious of that step from summer shade.

Gladdon

Upright Hedge-parsley

Strange that it is so rare about the Downs themselves - it likes the reassuring presence of the beech and its roots in chalk. Nonetheless in Sussex it is the most abundant Helleborine.

Butterflies need heat to warm their wings and food to feed their caterpillars. The local butterfly population relates in large part to the density of food plants. In this area we have extensive colonies of clover, Horseshoe Vetch, thistle, violet,

Broad-leaved Helleborine

scabious, Sloe and Dyer's Greenweed, to name but a few, which help support a range of species, some very local to the chalk, and often in good numbers. The Orange Tip lays its eggs singly at the base of a *cuckoo flower*. It is not wholly dependent on the plant for energy as the crawlers eat each other. The Green Hairstreak puts its eggs not on the leaves, but in the flowers of the Dyer's Greenweed, while the Red Admiral, shown here, lays eggs on the nettle, as do the Peacock and the Comma. The pink of Hemp Agrimony shows well against the breaking waves below. Said to prefer wet places but it seems successful, too, by the tracks and in the grassy hedgebanks where the soil is dry. The 'raspberries and cream' of its flower is a magnet for the butterflies. As they gorge on high-summer nectar they become drugged so that they can be touched and are happy to be handled. Another pinkish plant that punctuates the traveller's way is *wild rhubarb* -; pink-stemmed Burdock, a plant of cattle-trampled pasture, scrubby coombe, the mouth of badgers' dens and the rabbit warrens on the cliff. Burdock looks best when its flowers are newly opened and marbled white. Hooks on bracts, fruit walls and styles catch feather, hair and fur - a trick played by Enchanter's Nightshade, Forget-me-not, as well as Burdock. Hooks on seed-coats are very rare - indeed there is no British example. More rhubarby yet, the Ragwort stem.

Male Orange Tip

Broad-leaved Helleborine

Burdock's root is still in use: wilderness survivalists roast it, as you would a potato, in the embers of their fires. You will find it in Japanese restaurants finely sliced with carrot, then quick fried in sesame oil. Or drink it as a cordial. Previously the root was a poultice "for the bite of a mad dog" [C]. Stranger was its obstetric role: "by its leaf you may draw the womb which way you please, further upwards by applying it to the crown of the head ..., or downwards by applying it to the soles of the feet: or if you would it stay in its place apply it to the navel and that is likewise a good way to stay the child in it" [C].

Comma

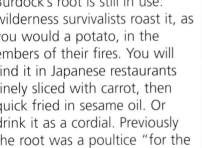

Red Admiral on Hemp Agrimony

Burdock

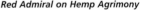

Ragwort stems

Here, too, in the Downland bottoms is the *enchanteresse*, for a syrop made against elf-sickness. To Gerard it was "inchanter's nightshade", a

Elecampane

Enchanter's Nightshade

Tuberous Pea

plant with a mysterious and magical name found not just in "obscure, dark places". True, you will find it on the mossy banks under the Sloe where only filtered sunlight penetrates, but do not be too surprised to see it in the open.

Near Firle lie the ancient ruins of an inn, where once travellers pulled up to rest and dine. An important stop, too, for the beasts of burden, be they mules or horses, to have any injuries attended to. Elecampane, which still grows there was likely planted as a horse medicine - another name was *horse-heal* and Inula, its generic name, might have derived from hinnulus - a mule. Like Soapwort, Tansy and some others, it was an import to the physic garden which afterwards broke out. It came from Asia as a panacea: used against the plague, asthma, convulsions and contusions. Rare too, this crimson pea, to which I make an annual pilgrimage, hoping to see it once again. Known as the Fyfield pea, from its presence in that Essex parish since 1800.

At the foot of High and Over together the benign and the malign grow together - the sweet Sea Milkwort and the deadly Hemlock. Purple-splashed stems, like the spreading rash of the meningococcus, intimate its danger. *Devil's blossom* turns to seed, rich in coniine, an alkaloid which can induce respiratory paralysis. Unlike some other alkaloid poisons, coniine does not induce confusion or hallucinosis: it

Hemlock

Hemlock

simply asphyxiates and those mottled stems, though less toxic than the seed, have sadly proved fatal as a child's whistle or a blow pipe.

Aromatic and with a most evocative name, Meadowsweet, a strowing plant: cast on stone and earthen floors to take the edge off insanitary smells. It marries

well with Purple Loosestrife: Meadowsweet is gentle, Loosestrife bold and they sit together by the Cuckmere. The latter's species name, Salicaria, refers to its willow-like foliage. In Medieval times Meadowsweet was used to lower fevers and, interestingly, its sap has subsequently been shown to contain chemicals of the same group as

Purple Loosestrife

salicylic acid, Aspirin, our most useful febrifuge. Meadowsweet is a corruption of mede-sweet from its use to flavour mead. Otherwise, it is *queen-of-the-meadow.* More common hereabouts in watery places is the Marsh Woundwort. Take a lens to the writing on its petals; relish the delicious scribbles - more poetry than in many poems. Gerard saw it

Meadowsweet

Marsh Woundwort

"in the meadowes by Lambeth". He tells of a Kentish man who cut his leg with a scythe, with the wound down to the bone and bleeding badly: "the poore man crept unto this herbe which he bruised with his hands and tied a great quantitie of it unto the wound with a piece of his shirt, which presently stanched the bleeding and

ceased the pain". This poultice which "did as it were glew, sodder the lips of the wound together ... was fully performed in seven daies". Gerard saw the wound himself and "offered to heal the same for charity: which he refused saying that I could

Frog Orchid

not heale it so well as himselfe: a clownish answer I confess without any thankes for my good will: whereupon I have named it Clownes Woundwort". But he was impressed - he subsequently used the Clownes Woundwort on "a gentleman of Grayes Inne in Holborn, Mr Edmund Cartwright, who was thrust into the lungs, the wound entering into the lower part of the thorax ... in so much that from day to day the frothing and puffing of the lungs did spew forth of the wound such excrement as it was possessed of ... I perfectly cured it in very short time, and with this Clownes experiment".

You will search hard to find the hollow-tongued orchid, Coeloglossum. Surprisingly, it is distributed through the whole of the British Isles, and in the north is more likely to be tinged maroon rather than pale green. It shows pugnacity growing on limestone to a thousand metres. A tiny orchid which needs the shortest turf or the shell sand of the Hebrides. There, among the Meadow Rue, where Scarp's rockets shot across the turquoise sound, it sits in heavenly peace. In Sussex, like the Musk Orchid, the secretive Frog Orchid follows the undulations of the Downs.

Betony

Burnet Saxifrage with Betony

Wild Geraniums, Betony and Burnet Saxifrage have by now emerged, all small herbs growing near the sea. Betony grows as high as Foxgloves in sheltered Cornish ditches, but here its ecotype is tiny - sometimes but an inch. Devil's-bit Scabious and Knapweed have similarly small ecotypes and will be major players later in the year. Betony, pink-flowered with a very handsome leaf: "indented about the edges like a saw" [G], was thought "a very precious herbe" [C] - "it helpeth those that piss or spit blood, them with weak stomachs and sour belchings" and was an aide to "an easy, speedy delivery in childbirth". The Long-stalked Crane's-bill is a geranium in miniature and, happily, quite common.

From hair-like flower stalks hang its miniature purple bells. Another magico-medicinal herb to which wounded animals were drawn. Beside it will likely be the unassuming Molle.

Long-stalked Crane's-bill

The Burnet Saxifrage is a lime-lover, one of the tiniest umbellifers and here it may average only 12 cm. The Burnet Rose derives its species name, Pimpinellifolia from the resemblance of its leaves to those of the Burnet Saxifrage - Pimpinella saxifraga, a member of the parsley family.

Dove's-foot Crane's-bill

Sussex holds the greatest numbers of Burnt Orchid in the country with the greatest concentraton found at this eastern end of Downland. The early-flowering form has already been described. This, the late-flowering variety, now in bloom, has a hood which retains its dark colour.

Burnt Orchid

Unlike Fool's Parsley, Ragwort remains poisonous when dried and is a menace to horses when it sullies hay. Cows seem to avoid it as they do with Buttercups, but sheep retard its growth by eating out the bud of its leaf rosette. The Cinnabar

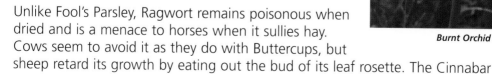

Cinnabar caterpillar

Ragwort

moth turns Ragwort's poison to its own advantage - its caterpillars feed off the plant accumulating toxin to deter their own predators. As one of five plants scheduled in the Weed Act of 1974, farmers attempt to pull it and keep its numbers down, but a tide of yellow ragwort under a hot, blue sky is too bonny to be denied. A ragged-leaved plant and from its tatters it got its name. In Highland folklore fairies flew on sticks of Ragweed from isle to isle and Burns' witches, too, had Ragweed nags -

"Let warlocks grim, an' wither'd Hags
Tell how wi'you on Ragweed nags
They skim the muirs an' dizzy crags
Wi' wicked speed".

When bees work Ragwort their wax is not the surprising white of muslin, rather a deep, deep yellow.

Battlefields and poppies, corn and poppies, thunder and poppies. Since the earliest agriculture corn was married to the Poppy, the *corn-rose*. Its "gallant red" came from the blood of soldiers, but its associations with death and resurrection reach back far beyond the Battle of the Somme. Pick the Poppy and you will bring on thunder, but put it in your roof to field off lightning. It was also, like the Tansy, a migraine plant. Poppy nectar seems to have a narcotic effect on bees, evident in their difficulty finding the hive entrance if they have drunk deep. Long-headed and Rough

Drifts of poppies

Long-headed Poppy *Long-headed Poppy* *Rough Poppy* *Common Poppy buds*

Rough Poppy

Poppies find anonymity in a sea of Common Poppies, but wade deep and trawl long for the powder-blue anthers of the occasional Rough Poppy.

The signature of the Milk Thistle is the white-veined leaf, splashed by the Virgin's milk as she suckled baby Jesus: in the 17th century these leaves were "a proper diet for wet nurses". Growing taller than a man it is somewhat shambling in its overall effect. As an introduction from Southern Europe it was more common in the 16th century than it is now, favouring, it seemed, the dunghill. I only know it in one site in these hills - oddly a featureless sheep pasture, but perhaps a midden stood there once. The bracts of the involucre can be eaten like an artichoke, but beware its piercing armour.

Strong magic springs from Agrimony's black root, kept in its fairy wand. Useful for illness, a wool dye, and a tea came from its leaf. Yellow for the jaundice, yellow for a dye. Culpeper recommended it for those with "foul, troubled and bloody water". Treatment also for colds - in Somerset the *lemonade flower* - its flowers made into a drink with oranges, lemons, ginger and sugar.

Milk Thistle

Piercing armour

Honeybees will work Wild Raspberry when other flowers have been spoiled - its pendulous flowers protect the nectar from the rain. Raspberry honey is for the connoisseur - the 'single malt' of honeys. Bees can collect the juice from ripe and over-ripe raspberries as they are thin-skinned - the source of so-called "red honey" reported from time to time. The pollen, like that of Bramble and Himalayan Balsam, is white. This is the protein store, 'bee bread' for the grubs. The pollen that is packed into cells in the brood chamber forms an astonishing colour matrix: Horse Chestnut yields brick red, Poppy black, Loosestrife green, Heather slate-grey, Ivy dull yellow and Red Dead Nettle a bright orange. White pollen on my bees is most likely off the Bramble as Wild Raspberry is not prolific in the Downland scrub and hedgebank. Like *fireweed* it springs from burnt-out scrub. Many so-called Wild Raspberries come from the seeds of cultivated kinds, which have been dropped by birds. Like the little fruits of Wild Strawberry they have an intense flavour and are worth picking. Until the 16th century it was the *hind*

Agrimony

berry, eaten by wild deer, when Gerard had it as the *raspis bush.*

From a snakeskin casing bursts the Greater Knapweed like a butterfly from its pupal shuck. *Half Mourners,* like the plant they drink from, will cast their seed upon the wind - unlike many other butterflies which lay eggs on specific plants the *Half Mourner* drops its eggs in flight. Thousands upon tens of thousands of pink-purple heads dehisce and the grassland will brim full through the rest of summer.

Tall plants are everywhere: Ragworts, Knapweeds, St John's Worts and Agrimony in greatest numbers. Spring gave us the shorter herbs but now colour flows among the longer grasses.

White Campion emits its faint nocturnal scent to encourage visits from the moths. But beware this death flower. Pick White Campion and your mother will die -

hence *mother-dee,* pick Red Campion and your father will die. It seems this lovely plant was spread by migratory Neolithic farmers: there is a good correlation between Neolithic settlements in Scotland and the

White Campion

Raspberry and Wild Clematis

distribution of Wild Campion. Man's activities have determined the landscape

Greater Knapweed

Half Mourners

Chicory

White Horehound

Tutsan

Strawberries in chalk scree

Feverfew

and the flora of the chalklands. The Iron Age saw the retreat of chalk woodland. More recently, during the Napoleonic Wars, large acreages of chalk turf were converted into tillage with the soaring price of corn. When the war was over corn prices collapsed and ploughed downland was allowed to relapse to pasture. The old shepherds called early regenerating tall coarse grasses "gratton grass": grasses which choke and smother, sour places without interest.

Chicory and White Horehound, both chalk lovers and both grown for use; the former in the herb garden, the latter in the physic garden. Chicory's blue flowers are opened by the sun. Its root was a coffee substitute and in coffee blends it is a taste enhancer. The "sullen" [C] leaves of Horehound were used to expel the placenta and "bruised and boiled in old hog's grease into an ointment" used to heal any dirty wound inflicted by a dog.

The physic garden was on the way out by the mid-19th century: by then few apothecaries maintained such gardens or foraged in the woods for their prescriptions. Their source was now a wholesale medicinal herb business: plants grown to order in large volume. This was developed by the Shakers who arrived in the United States around the time of Independence (1770s). By 1826 more than 400 medicinal species were grown, gathered, processed and packed exclusively for physicians and pharmacists. The benefits were clear: most important, it was a big step towards a consistent product. In the 19th century Belladonna and Digitalis were farmed in England and Valerian in Belgium. By 1910 the United States had established experimental herb-growing farms for native plants approaching extinction. They also aimed to reduce the need for expensive foreign imports of plants such as Gentian. In 1918 there was a major crisis: an overproduction in the United States of belladonna caused the collapse of the US herb growing business. The belladonna operation was colossal: hundreds of acres planted in a single field and huge drying sheds were erected to cure the plant.

Another plant grown commercially as a fever cure and as an emmenagogue was Feverfew. Originally a plant of the Balkan mountains, it was hunted and brought across the Channel. As a headache cure the leaves were pulverised and piled upon the crown of the head. But physic went beyond symptoms and diseases, it could be cosmetic, it could modify feeling and behaviour. Tutsan was taken to be Pliny's Agnus Castus, long associated with chastity. Pliny advised women wishing to be chaste how they best lie upon it. As for men, always more of a therapeutic challenge in these matters, "it destroyeth and drywyth awey fowle lust of lecherye if men drinke it". In Normandy it is *tout-saine,* all wholesome, in Sussex, *sweet amber:* its dried leaves were thought to smell of ambergris and for their scent, as well as luck, they were put between the pages of the Bible.

Plethoric? - it's the Wild Strawberry for you: Gerard vows it "will take away the rednesse of the face". These little gems peek from woodland banks, quarry slopes and cliff-top heaths: Downland gardens of earthly delight - they inhabit, too, Hieronymus Bosch's fantastical Garden of Earthly Delights, as a symbol of eroticism.

Wild Strawberry slope

Black seeds from the Medick and Cow Wheat. Black Medick, quite different from the Hop Trefoil in fruit, creeps among Cat's-ear, Flax and Carrot. Unusually, the kidney-shaped seed pods do not split open to release the seed, instead seed germinates inside the protective pod. Once formed its rootlets push through the wall to continue the growing cycle. Melampyrum is in the open woodlands below the scarp - it favours lime-poor soil.

Cow Wheat   *Spotted Medick*

Some cow-wheats parasitise cereals: so, an unwelcome corn-field plant. On the Isle of Wight contaminated wheat was milled to make so-called "poverty bread". Chalk was used widely in the past by unscrupulous bakers to adulterate their flour just as talc is used to eke out cocaine.

Common Mallow

Malva Neglecta

The flat, cake-shaped nutlets of the Common Mallow are like little cheeses and have a nutty flavour. In France they are called *fromage* and in Sussex *cheese flowers*. All the mallows are mucilaginous and thus suited for making poultices, eg, by boiling barley flour as the base. Such poultices were applied to various inflammations including "swelling of the cods" and other hot tumours. The mallows' temper is bold and bright but there is a little mallow, Malva neglecta, which is prone, pale and shy. Like Fat Hen,

Hare's-foot Clover

Silverweed and Nettle it follows human settlement, where there is spoil, rich in nitrogen. In car parks and on wasteland the neglected Mallow will be trampled, gone unseen. But on the foreshore driftline it is in a seaside garden of Hare's-foot Clover, Red Hemp-nettle, Sea Campion, Chicory and Bittersweet.

"Lagopus", as was, now Hare's-foot, is the bonniest of clovers. The Red Hemp-nettle is very local and I have seen it only on the shingle although it also grows amongst arable crops on dry chalk soils. Bittersweet's green eggs and Sea Campion, a dainty seaside "tumbleweed" lie among the pebbles. Tumbleweeds occur mainly in Steppe or desert areas - the whole or part of the plant is carried by the wind to broadcast its seed.

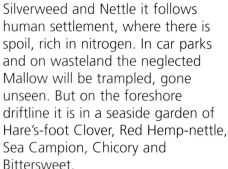

Red Hemp-nettle

Bittersweet's green fruits

Sea Campion

Marsh dwelling plants now in flower include Creeping Jenny, Sea Milkwort, Water Forget-me-not, Water Speedwell, Water Plantain and the Greater Bird's-foot Trefoil. The Water Plantain was originally a native of North America. The settlers found the application of its blistering leaves drew water from dropsical legs, so they called it *water suck-leaves*. The tiny Sea Milkwort is in the brackish flats near the Cuckmere's mouth. A pink petalless, stalkless gem. It grows, too, on the shell sand of Berneray where Dunlin and Ringed Plover conceal their chicks in the crofters' strips of rye and barley, tinged blue by Bugloss and gashed with the astonishing yellow of Corn Marigold. Just west of Lewes, near

Creeping Jenny

Water Speedwell

Greater Bird's-foot Trefoil

Ditchling, *yellow gold* grows with Night-flowering Catchfly on the arable margins of a Downland top: but that is a two day walk from here. Further upstream on muddy banks over which a stream is prone to spill grows Creeping Jenny and the Water Forget-me-not. A drowning knight threw these flowers to his lover, calling desperately as he was dragged under, "forget me not" - since then to wear it guarantees you will not be forgotten by your love. Opening buds are pink and the transition to a glorious sky-blue is gradual. Its petals contain anthocyanins and so the cellular pH determines colour. It reproduces vegetatively from rooting stem fragments.

Water Plantain

Natural ponds, and likewise village ponds, are rare along this stretch of Downland but find still water and you will find some plants of interest. Dew-ponds are often choked these days. The Downland shepherds prefer to call them sheep ponds and in other counties they were known as fog-ponds, cloud-ponds or mist-ponds. In 1923 Arthur Beckett met an old man called Weller,

Sea Milkwort

Hebridean Corn Marigold

Water Forget-me-not

then over 80, who worked on the Glynde estate and had spent 60 years constructing dew-ponds on the Downs. Asked how he used to construct a dew-pond the ancient looked perplexed and shook his head. Beckett tried "sheep-ponds" - "Oh, ship-ponds", he said, "I didn't know what you meant when you talked about dew-ponds". Sited mostly on the summits of the higher hills, they were used for watering the sheep and cattle. The obvious question is how were they

New Zealand Pigmyweed

Greater Spearwort

supplied with water as there are no springs and they are built into such porous rock with no appreciable supply of surface water that can top them up. It seems that even in the driest summers they were never empty. Water came from mist, from sea fogs and from rain. Weller and his grandfather followed the same method of construction: once hollowed to a good depth the excavation was covered by a layer of mortar into which a course of flints was rammed. Eventually there were two courses of mortar and two courses of flint in alternating layers, topped off with "a comp" of plaster and sea sand. Prior to that method, Sussex oxen trampled clay, then flints were layered, then more clay trampled in. In other constructions straw was used between layers of lime-tempered clay and broken chalk. Most modern ones were made with two layers of concrete. Straw was incorporated as an insulator, keeping the warmth of the earth from the water. Now many dew-ponds are in disrepair and some are brimful with weed, including the unwelcome New Zealand Pigmyweed. It was first recorded from Essex in 1956 and has since appeared in a number of localities from Sussex to Argyll.

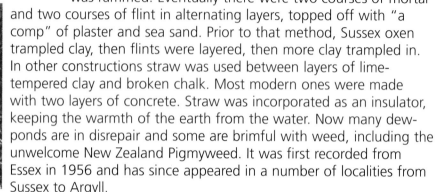

Apart from puddling dew-ponds, oxen were the means of hauling timber across the claggy weald. Defoe recorded a team of 22 drawing a massive oak tree to the sawyer. The last working team was at Exceat Farm, near Eastbourne, in 1927. The Sussex ox could not be shod in the simple way of a horse: it had to be thrown on its back with the ox-herd sitting on its neck then a wooden tripod was placed over the beast to which its legs were tied for shoeing.

Friston pond holds Greater Spearwort and the White Water-lily. Man-high Greater Spearwort is the tallest Buttercup boasting splendid flaggy leaves and the White Water-lily is Britain's largest wild flower. Its root was cropped by the Hebrideans for a black dye. Lilies can be so numerous there as to pave a lochan. This can severely hamper the travel of the fly-line on the surface. So

White Water-lily

thick are the stems that if your fly engages, your cast is almost always lost. Its numbers have suffered from profiteering: but most bloom unseen over the tiny trout that make the leaves their shelter, as on the lost lochans under Suilven's dome. There small beetles carry round the lilies' pollen.

Fringed Water-lily and Amphibious Bistort are infrequent in Downland's watery places. Bistort, twice-twisted, refers to its contorted stems. It can live in water or on land and when on land its leaves sprout hairs it lacks on water.

Where salt marsh blends into shingle many plants have successfully met the harsh environmental challenge. Glasswort is a succulent, Red Bartsia has its hairy cloak and Narrow-leaved Bird's-foot Trefoil a slender leaf.

Fringed Water-lily

Amphibious Bistort

Red Bartsia, drear and dusty, but in the paddocks at Jevington it makes bright heather-coloured clumps. Some genera, eg, Gentiana, have very similar species which flower in spring or autumn respectively. Genus Odontites, the Red Bartsia genus, provide the best example locally. O.vernus flowers in spring and summer while the subspecies serotinus waits till later in the year. Glasswort, like a green translucent coral has many-jointed stems,

Red Bartsia

Glasswort

Narrow-leaved Bird's-foot Trefoil

each segment putting out several tiny flowers. Its plump sprigs are still gathered in East Anglia where they are turned to pickle. At low tide it was gathered to be burnt for its ash, high in soda and of use in glassmaking. (It

Sea Beet

Sea Lavender

Purple Toadflax

Broad-leaved Everlasting Pea

Hoary Stock

Branched Bur-reed

did yield only a poor quality of glass so it was superseded when purer forms of soda became available.) The Narrow-leaved Bird's-foot Trefoil is a very local species of South East England found on short, brackish grassland or on the tight shingle where the turf begins.

Each Sea Lavender plant will produce comparatively few seeds, roughly 400, while a Foxglove will run to 750,000. A stone's throw from the marsh sea-grasses flower and release their pollen-grains under water. Zostera's thread-like pollen is of the same specific gravity as the seawater so neither sinks nor rises - it floats at the level of its release which is where the stigma waits. A number of Sea Lavenders are among the small number of endemic British species - there are some fifteen or so, including a strange cabbage-like plant confined to Lundy Island.

Sea Beet's root is rich in sugar, as you would expect of a close relative of the sugar beet.

Where the shingle is banked up Purple Toadflax, White Stonecrop and Broad-leaved Everlasting Pea - purple, white and pink - nestle in the hollows. Hoary Stock grows, white-petalled, below the cliff at Holywell, nicely scented as a stock should be. At Brighton, where there is a better known colony, white forms have seemingly reverted to the commoner deep pink. The first UK record of this plant came from Hastings in 1806.

Branched Bur-reed grows beside exotic Bladderwort. Zig-zag stems end in flowering spikes carrying many little balls of flower. The female heads sport beaked fruits which confer the bur-like look. Both male and female flowers are simple: no need for show as the plant is wind pollinated. Bladderwort is rootless and insectivorous. Its tiny underwater leaves have air-filled bladders and when touched by an insect the bladder opens and sucks it in. Some insectivores, like Butterwort, secrete digestive enzymes to break down prey but the Bladderwort takes the longer view, produces no such juices and absorbs the soluble products of decomposition. Once done the bladder opens and water is pumped out and again the trap is sprung. This is a very local plant, found at both ends of this stretch of Downland, in the Pevensey Levels and in the ditches of Southease.

Bladderwort

Melilot and Woodruff are rich in coumarin, an aromatic substance which gives the smell of new-mown hay. Because of coumarin Melilot is toxic to grazing animals but otherwise is good for green manure. The yellow form, a naturalised alien, is widespread on road verges and in shingle; the white form is quite infrequent hereabouts.

Moth Mullein

Ribbed Melilot

White Melilot

One of six mullein species, Moth Mullein is a declining species and very local. Originally native to Southern Europe, the Near East and North Africa it is usually yellow, but all of the plants in this site are of a rarer white. Only one flower grows from each bract.

A pale grassland beauty, the Hoary Plantain. Silver of stem, lilac in its stamens, white on its anthers and its petals. This is the only

Hoary Plantain

Bladder Campion

Hairy Buttercup

scented plantain, the others have no need of insects. In Devon they call it *scent bottles.* Insects are drawn, too, by the Bladder Campion: but its nectaries are unusually deep and inaccessible. At dusk the plant puts out more scent, but even long-tongued moths struggle to reach the prize. Luminous, bifid petals stream from its inflated, purple-veined calyx, like a piece of cloudy glassware by Lalique. Crafty Bumblebees who will forage when the Honeybee is hivebound by wind and rain have found an easier way: biting through the flower to draw its nectar. As to its scent, it smells of garden peas.

At the foot of "High and Over" in damp ditches near the sea Hairy Buttercups like to crowd, and viewed from high they mark out long bars of yellow in the pasture. Dry chalk banks are yellowed, too, by unidentified Asteraceae: Hawk's-beards, Hawkbits, Hawkweeds...

Enter the *King's taper*. The upward pointing leaves of Great Mullein funnel moisture to its roots. Though most of its parts are poisonous the herbalists put it to good use. Culpeper reckoned Mullein was good for the flaming joints of gout. Its flowering stems suggested torches, flames and candles. Its great stalks were dipped in suet and fired up at funerals and other ceremonials. The down was scraped off its leaves and made into candlewicks: hence its names *candlewick plant* and *high taper*. Even the flowers were put to use as a yellow hair dye. Mullein likely relates to mollis, meaning soft, hence the *poor man's flannel*. But this *donkey's ear* is packed with chemical deterrents such as rotenone, the insecticide, and coumarin.

Some plants make their presence known by putting out a pungent smell. *Stinking Roger* is one such plant. Its smell is a deterrent to cattle which might otherwise devour it. Another moniker of Black Horehound is *madwort* as it was used to treat the bites of rabid dogs. It forms great clumps, often in a tangle amongst the Honeysuckle, the Bramble and the Elder. Its lower lip is stencilled white.

A more complex hieroglyph, read only by the insects, is on the Common Hemp-nettle. Like the imprint of a mythic butterfly, etched purple and suffused with yellow.

In late July *Half Mourners* are on Wild Basil, pale grasses are throwing seed and glinting flints are baking in the dessicating chalk. Heat and high summer's wayside plants are the traveller's companions: Mugworts, Melilots and Mallows, while in the thickets and the hedges Honeysuckle and Traveller's Joy. The Wayfaring berries have almost gone to red. July was the time when the wheatear was most plentiful. The origin of its name is Anglo-Saxon, meaning white-rump. Its numbers now are much reduced. Sussex, according to a proverb, is celebrated for

Great Mullein

Marbled White

seven culinary delights: a Selsey cockle, a Chichester lobster, an Arundel mullet, an Amberley trout, a Pulborough eel, a Rye herring and a Bourne (Eastbourne) wheatear: the most delectable of those was the Bourne Wheatear. It feeds on insects, snails, grubs and beetles and is fattest when the wheat is ripe. For hundreds of years it had been a table delicacy know as the "English ortolan". Shepherds were able to supplement their income by trapping the birds for sale. Their way of trapping Wheatears was peculiar: a series of T-shaped shallow trenches, each about a foot

Wayfaring Tree's berries

Wild Basil

Black Horehound

long, was dug on the slope of a Down. A horsehair spring was set at the inner end, then the sod replaced on the top of the trap, grass downwards. There was a small entrance left by which the bird would enter. Its habit is to skim the ground in flight and if at all alarmed it seeks the nearest shelter. It was said that even the shadow of a cloud would spook the Wheatear. Often on these open Downs the nearest hiding place would be a cranny in the ground. The Downs were honeycombed with these peculiar coops and a single shepherd might capture 90 dozen Wheatears in a year. In 1842 sixty dozen Wheatears were sent to London by the Eastbourne coach. According to "the Compleat History of Sussex" (1730) "Eastbourne, (Eborn) although found on our maps is only drawn to the attention of a reader on account of its being chief place of catching the delicious birds called Wheatears which much resemble the French ortolans".

Field Milk-thistle

..... and ever the Yaffle

Common Hemp-nettle

August

Over gentle Downland a gull-white cumulus fakes a towering peak. But here the hills are modest. Over them and round them snake the tracks that bore the pilgrim, along which Neolithic men ferried their dead - each making their different journey to the after-life. Better to look away from illusory goals, the tops you will never reach, instead look down at the flowers by your feet - enjoy the journey, forget arrival.

It is after a severe summer storm that the effect of salt spray is most evident, particularly so if hot, dry weather follows. Then, the less tolerant plants will show signs of scorching. Characteristic maritime heath plants are Bird's-foot Trefoil, Eyebright, Wild Thyme and Tormentil. Towards the cliff edge high levels of salt deposition inhibit heather growth, which is to the advantage of plants like Buck's-horn Plantain and Red Fescue.

Two miles inland, at Lullington Heath, Bell Heather engulfs the slopes. Encroachment by scrub is carefully controlled and in recent years Exmoor ponies as well as goats have been introduced with that in mind. Here short-rooted acid lovers and long-rooted chalk lovers grow in an unusual community

Carline Thistle

of plants. How remarkable - a Carline Thistle in a bed of Heather.

Heather, like Hawthorn, is fickle in its nectar yield and it is said that Heather on chalk, rare though it be, is grudging to the honeybee. Early in the morning various nectars may be low in sugar, but as the day warms up the sugar content can quadruple through evaporation. The bees may forgo nectar on cool days, particularly in the morning, and concentrate on pollen gathering. They will also favour a plant with an open flower construction as this allows more rapid evaporation and concentration of the nectar. Honeybees expend a lot of energy and time on

nectar concentration in the hive: only when the water content is low enough to prevent fermentation will they cap

Bell Heather

Ling

the honey in its cell. The poor economy of the Highlands and Islands, particularly at the times of the Clearances, when sheep supplanted townships, turned heather into thatch, a bedding, a fuel, a rope, a dye and a flavouring for beer. For tethering animals rope was made from rushes, from straw for thatching stacks, and from heather for securing thatch on buildings. Yet greater strength was needed for ropes used in ploughing, for which root fibres

were used. Horse-hair ropes could be twisted into thick cables and were used, for example, to lower fowlers down the cliffs. Many evicted Highlanders were forced to flee to North America and, needless to say, they took their Heather with them. The Carline is universal through our Downland: by tracks, on heaths, in the fine turf, even clinging to the bare seaside chalk. In its first season it is a flat, prickly rosette of leaves,

Heather on the cliff

Carline Thistle

only putting out its stem in the second year of growth. Through the winter it is an everlasting flower. The flower heads close in damp and open in the dry. Its florets are of a gorgeous purple while stiff silvery bracts give it a starburst head. Its name, a corruption of Charlemagne, arose from the plague infecting the king's army. He prayed to God for help - as a result of which an angel directed him to shoot an arrow. Whichever plant was struck would cure the plague - none other than this thistle.

Bells of blue tied in a posy: a scarce jewel of the chalk, the Clustered Bellflower. Tiny on the windiest slopes, a foot taller on a sheltered site. As with any plant with red in its stem it was regarded with suspicion: likely a corpse plant sucking blood up from the dead - hence known as *Dane's blood*. These Bellflowers are most numerous in the cliff turf on the leeward side, in the shelter of the Privet and the Furze.

Clustered Bellflower

Another small blue plant well adapted to the dryness on quick draining chalk is the Small Scabious. Its muted blue suggested the colour of a dove and hence the second part of its botanical name, columbaria.

For those who travel to these gentle canyons full of flowers the Wild Parsnip is a high point in the procession of our summer plants. Pastinaca sativa, meaning something dug from the ground - though Gerard

A favourite of the Burnet Moth

Small Scabious

thought it not worth the digging: "small, hard, woodie and not fit to be eaten". Scrolled petals on its flowers which are massed in greeny-yellow umbels. Its leaves are stuffed with the smell of parsnip and, like heather, it was used for flavouring by the brewer.

Legend has it that Vervain grew on Calvary and was used to staunch Christ's bleeding wounds after He was taken off the cross. And so it became a holy plant. To the Romans it was an altar plant, likely used in sacrificial ceremonies. As one would expect from its Biblical association, it was invested with great healing power - a top to tail treatment - from mental illness, ("good for those that are frantic") to haemorrhoids. You will see it here and there, not in great numbers, along chalk paths and on dry woodland rides - architectural, small flowered and open in design. Akin to the Hedge Mustard in the composition of its stems, rendering a hazy effect by a suspension of pale and misty lilac flowers.

Wild Parsnip

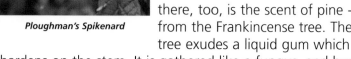
Ploughman's Spikenard

Ploughman's Spikenard, like Vervain, is an occasional companion as I make my way across the chalk. It pushes through the Basil and the Bramble in forgotten spots. Spikenard was a valuable Indian perfume ranked with myrrh and frankincense. Frankincense is pine-scented. When I think of pine the ancient woods of Caledonia, Mediterranean seashores and Californian forests come to mind, but in the bareness of the Yemeni desert there, too, is the scent of pine - from the Frankincense tree. The tree exudes a liquid gum which hardens on the stem. It is gathered like a fungus, and burns with a fragrant smoke which wafts men's prayers to heaven. Spikenard came from a Himalayan plant and spawned various less costly substitutes. Downland folk hung its roots about their cottages to freshen the air, rather as Meadowsweet was used about the floor. A poorman's spikenard, the Ploughman's Spikenard. In

Vervain

Hedge Mustard

conjunction with Field Penny-cress it was used as a mithridate, an antidote to poison. The strange concept of building immunity to a poison by ingesting ever increasing amounts came from Mithradates (120-63 BC), King of Pontus (Crimea).

Yarrow

Wild Basil was another strowing herb, aromatic and gentle. It is a plant favoured by butterflies and will last long into autumn: sometimes it flowers past the Ragwort, as does Yarrow. Yarrow was for those wounded with iron and carries its signature in its leaf; a thousand cuts - hence millefolium. In France and Ireland a plant with magical powers, a herb of St John. On St John's Eve the Irish hang it in their homes to ward off illness. Contrariwise, the Devil's plant: *old man's mustard, old man's pepper,* 'old man' being the devil. It was a plant, too, of elves and goblins, for harming others. Here is a Gaelic incantation which illustrates its double edge - "I will pick the smooth yarrow that my figure may be sweeter, that my lips may be warmer, that my voice may be gladder. May my voice be like a sunbeam, may my lips be like the juice of a strawberry. May I be an island in the sea, may I be a hill in the land, may I be a star in the dark time, may I be a staff to the weak one: I shall wound every man, no man shall hurt me" The tension between the pagan and the Christian 'ownership' of plants, consequently the powers held by plants, is evident in their names - a saintly plant but also a devilish one, a force for good yet a force for evil.

Field Scabious

Tall above the Yarrow blow the blue heads of Field Scabious, a useful plant to caterpillars, notably of the Chalkhill Blue. I am puzzled this butterfly has not taken stronger hold as it is well suited to the dryness of this climate. This plant has a clever trick to prevent self-pollination - the stamens wither before the ripening of the stigma. The wort for itch, scabies and tetters and a head-wash for scurf and dandruff. It is also one of the few plants mentioned as a cure for leprosy in the English Herbaria.

Dark Mullein can reach head height but is never the imposing plant Great

Teasel

Mullein is. It restricts itself to the blots on our landscape such as supermarket car parks. It should stretch its legs over the Downs where it would look very well. Another plant of wasteground is the Teasel. Happily, it grows, too, in many scenic spots. Water collects at the leaf bases where insects become trapped and drown. The Romans called it *Venus' basin* as the collected water was applied as a cosmetic "to render the face fair" [C]. The *manured teasel* was cultivated in Culpeper's time when cloth workers used its wiry head to card their fabric. Its flowers have an unusual progression of opening: a central ring of blossom spreads upwards and downwards simultaneously. It deserves a fine setting: ideally a shingle bank, reddened with Spur Valerian and in earshot of the crashing waves. With narrower leaflets and a smaller terminal lobe, Hoary Ragwort is somehow handsomer than the common form, and with flowers, too, that look a little finer. A prettier

yellow yet belongs to the Evening Primroses which mass to form great regiments along the roads of counties to our west. However, it is not much seen in our road verges - more likely in a cottage garden, a disused chalk pit

Dark Mullein

or wastelands around Newhaven. It is a relative of the willowherbs and, like them, it has a close association with night flying moths. Its unfurling bud is worth a close examination. By it you will likely find the Soapwort - both like a site of former industrial activity, in particular textile manufacture. Soapwort flourishes at Tidemills among the flotsam behind the shingle bank. Brought in from abroad for industrial use it was once a commercial crop. Grown close to woollen mills, its stems were crushed and boiled in water to cleanse wool and linen. A liquid soap can be obtained quite simply by boiling its leaves. Saponins are released when the plant is crushed which cause it to foam in water. Some saponins have an antibiotic effect and it may be that they give the plant some

Evening Primrose

Hoary Ragwort

protection against damaging soil fungi. Anthocyanins, plant pigments, also defend against plant pathogens by inhibiting the growth of microbes.

Prior to Gerard only three species of native English thistle were recorded. His recordings of the Spear Thistle and the Nodding Thistle were the first. Both handsome, the former staunch, the latter gentle and demure.

Soapwort

Spear Thistle

William Withering published his "Account of the Foxglove" in 1785. In it he describes how he had obtained, from a woman in Shropshire, a complex recipe to cure dropsy, a swelling of the legs consequent on a failing heart. With persistence and only the simplest pieces of equipment he made an important contribution to pharmacology. The Foxglove is a poisonous plant containing glycosides (some thirty including digoxin, digitoxin and digitonin). Some of these glycosides act on cardiac muscle to make a weakened heart contract more forcefully. These compounds also have an effect on the electrical conducting system of the heart and can be used to slow the heart rate down when it goes dangerously fast. Paradoxically, this was one of the rare plants that Gerard pronounced to be "of no use" medicinally. Culpeper used it for the "King's Evil", tuberculosis. He also recommended an ointment made from it as one of the best remedies for a scabby head. With its bell-shaped flowers it was inevitably invested with magic and myth: in Celtic folklore foxglove juice could be used to get rid of a changeling. Also known as *bee-catchers, dead men's thimbles, long purples* and in Gaelic as *dead old woman's paps.* Withering realised that the therapeutic dose was close

Foxglove

to the toxic dose and it continues a difficult drug to use for that reason. Vincent van Gogh's epilepsy was treated with digitalis. It may be that the yellow circles round the stars in his "Starry Night" represent the visual disturbances he actually experienced through overmuch digoxin. It was used as a symbolic plant in Medieval Christian art, for example Panitir (Prado, 15th century) had foxglove in the foreground as the Virgin mother suckled baby Jesus. The Purple Foxglove was long used in herbal medicine but it is the Woolly Foxglove that was field cropped in Holland for digoxin. While many plants were used as panaceae whether the patient had filthy sores, spitting of blood, torments of the guts or stinking fistulas, some of the very early specific applications of medicinal plants were subsequently scientifically validated. Dioscorides, an army doctor in the first century AD, advocated a decoction of White Willow for gout. Salicylic acid is in the willow and it was only in 1899 that it was synthesised in a laboratory. Other important medicines of the 20th century were derived from plants long before being synthesised. Lignocaine, the local anaesthetic, was originally derived from gramine, an alkaloid in barley. That was not synthesised until 1935. Observations of the adverse effects of certain plants on animals have also led to specific pharmacological therapies. Most of the major anti-thrombotic drugs derive from veterinary practice in the 1920s when cattle were seen to develop stomach haemorrhages from eating hay contaminated by Melilot: whence synthetic dicoumarol (Warfarin) was born. Other toxic plant substances have been turned into medicines. The photosensitising compound methoxsalen derived from the blistering plants Rue and Giant Hogweed now bring relief to psoriatics and sufferers of skin lymphoma when coupled to ultraviolet exposure in a tanning cabinet.

Fennel

Rarely seen above the Weald, Fennel is a local plant in Downland, a handsome herb that likes sea air. It is naturalised all about the roads in Eastbourne but I have never seen it deep in Downland. Likely it was a naturalised physic herb and is now a pot herb. Similarly, Buddleja is widely naturalised, but seems more at home on a railway embankment or some ruinous spot, near habitation, rather than in a Downland hedge. And so with Tansy.

A native maritime species, the Tree Mallow and built for gales. It keeps its leaves in winter and when the stalks go limp in frost it has a paralytic look about it. Out in the Atlantic it clings to the granite of St Agnes' shore just short of the flash from the lighthouse on Bishop Rock.

Buddleja

The association between Mugwort and the travelling man goes back to ancient times: Pliny said "the wayfaring man that hath the herb tied about him feeleth no wearisomness at all". Easily overlooked as dusty, like the traveller himself, in fact the finely cut leaves are quite lovely - light on top, hoary-white below. In the Middle Ages throughout Europe it was another of St John's plants, hung over doors to ward off "wycked sprytes" after its purification in the bonfire smoke of St John's Eve. In Anglo-Saxon times it was said to secrete a "coal" between its roots on Midsummer's Eve: if dug this brought protection against lightning and the plague. Its smell is unattractive - it reminds me of interminable sermons, hard pews and the very old lady by whom, as a boy, I was always made to sit - she wore a 'scent' of old turnip crushed with mothball. However, the French will stuff a goose with aromatic Mugwort. Medicinally, Culpeper used it as an antidote to "the over-much taking of opium" and its juice was used as an abortifacient. In the Cuckmere estuary, Wormwood thrives with its feet in salt. Unlike so many of the worts, whose medicinal use has lapsed, Wormwood has yielded an active substance, artemisinin, which has been validated as a treatment for malaria. Previously it gave the bitter principle for absinthe, the quaff of the French impressionists. Its oils are repulsive to hive bees so a scrub of Wormwood on the hands helps keep the stingers off. It was used in the past against wax moth, whose larvae can devastate stored combs but is now outmoded. Older bee-keepers would stroke a bee cluster with a bruised Wormwood frond to shift an awkwardly located swarm, making it easier to coax into a skep.

Tansy

Mugwort

Tree Mallow

Wormwood

Rock Sea Lavender

Strawberry Clover

Sea Rocket

Take the path along the cliffs, Fulmars on the wing, they soar and dip to mock your slow ascents. Then, bored, they peel away. The track transports you, skirting fissures by the edge, to find Rock Sea Lavender only a salty gust from the marbled surge below. Just by it, peeps Strawberry Clover in the short, salt-burned grass. Sea Rocket is more likely seen on dunes or the driftline of a sandy beach, but here it is on shingle, just one clump from a single seed thrown by an angry sea. Widely dispersed around the UK coastline it often grows with Sea Sandwort. Sea Heath is a very local plant to coastal South East England, reaching round from Gibraltar Point in Lincolnshire to the Isle of Wight. Here it is at the northern limit of its distribution - it grows more freely in South West Europe. The Greater Sea Spurrey and its sticky-haired lookalike, Sand Spurrey, are hereabouts. The former likes the drier parts of the salt marshes at Cuckmere Haven. Further east on the shingle of Eastbourne's harbour is a big colony of Sticky Groundsel. The groundsels take their name from Old English "ground swallower" - anyone who works a vegetable patch knows why. They have a very short reproductive cycle and very efficient seed dispersal. Some plants can flower only if exposed to light for less than twelve hours (short-day plants), while others need sixteen hours of daylight (long-day plants) to be brought to the flowering stage. Groundsel is indifferent to the length of daylight so can flower in any month. "The flower of this herbe hath whyte hayre and when the wind bloweth it awaye then it appeareth like a bald headed man, therefore it is called senecio". This particular one, Sticky Groundsel, has a noxious smell and is extremely oily to the touch. However, on shingle a colony is not displeasing to the eye. But on wasteground amongst rusting metal, leaking batteries and sun-bleached plastic bottles it fails to thrill. Those are the places for the Dark Mullein.

Sea Sandwort

A black dye can be extracted from the odourless mint, Gipsywort, a dye that would hold fast in linen or in silk.

Greater Sea Spurrey

Sea Heath

More exotically, it was the fortune-teller's greasepaint as Threlkeld, 1727, described: "some call this the Gipsy-herb because those strolling cheats called Gipsies do dye themselves of a blackish hue with the juice of this plant, the better to pass for Africans by their tanned looks, and swarthy hides, to babble the credulous and ignorant by the practice of magick and fortune telling". A plant of marsh and streamside it grows, too, in peat and was a valued dye plant in the Inner Hebrides. Its saw-toothed leaves and its flowers flecked with

Sticky Groundsel

purple thrive in the wet clays at Downland's skirts. Corky rings surround its nutlets to give them buoyancy and so they cross the swampy ground.

Saw-wort

On the coastal heaths of South West England the Saw-wort can be small, but below these hills in the protected woodland it can be tall and bushy. It commended itself as a wound therapy by its saw-toothed leaf. Its second name, tinctoria, marks it as a dye plant. Its leaves give a greenish-yellow colour, similar to that of weld, which was suitable for dying woollens.

Gipsywort

Great Willowherb

By Gipsywort in these marshy spots grow Great Willowherb, Common Fleabane and Cudweed. The Great Willowherb is a very successful plant which will make a ditch its own. Its petal margin is slightly "snipt". Burn the Fleabane to dispel the fleas. Each flower head can contain up to 600 compressed florets, whence the Gatekeeper draws nectar. On chalky banks Blue Fleabane sits with Yellow-wort. Cudweed or *quidweed,* a tiny wee thing of muddy woodlands tracks was put in the mouths of cattle who had lost their cud. *Herbe impious* or

Fleabane

Fool's Watercress

Cudweed

Water Mint

wicked cudweede to Gerard: "bicause the yonger, or those flowers that spring up later, are higher, and over top those that come first, as many wicked children do unto their parents" - hence *son-afore-the-father,* its Scottish name.

The ditches and draining channels of the Cuckmere watermeadows brim with blossom at this time of year. The Heron's wing brushes Water Mint then Fool's Watercress as it spears its prey. This fool's plant sprawls and often ends up in a tangle. Its short-stalked flower heads are very characteristic, as is the arrangement of its leaflets, which are neatly paired. Also known as *pie-crest* its strong celery smell led West Country folk to put it in their pies. Water Mint, another fragrant strowing herb which "rejoiceth the hart of man" according to Gerard. He described how it was particularly used in places of recreation and "where feasts and banquets are made".

Touch-me-not, the cry of the balsams: capsules pop to eject their seeds at the merest pressure. Noli-me-tangere, from the words Christ spoke to Mary Magdalene after the Resurrection, is our only native species. The Orange Balsam is found by Michelham Priory. The Indian Balsam was

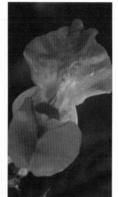

Blue Fleabane

Gatekeeper

Indian Balsam

originally a greenhouse introduction in 1839 but took little time to colonise our waterways.

Now, three of our most decorative water plants flower simultaneously - Arrowhead, Frogbit and Flowering Rush. Arrowhead, like Frogbit, is a three-petalled work of art. Not just its leaves are arrow-shaped, but its anthers, too. The flowers are hung on a whorled and leafless stem, and at the centre of each flower is a delicious purple stain. Not all leaves are aerial, some are floating and some are submerged.

De'l Obel was a contemporary of Gerard, had studied medicine at Montpellier, and later came to England to become botanist to James I. He was responsible for more than eighty "first records" of our native plants, amongst which are Grass-of-Parnassus, Deadly Nightshade and

Frogbit

Arrowhead

exotic Arrowhead. Gerard knew this plant as the *water archer;* he had found Sagittaria in the Tower ditch.

De'l Obel also first recorded the flowering rush and named it "Juncus soiperoides floridus paludosus"; the rush with leaves like a Coiperous and with flowers, which grows in marshy places. Gerard liked to think of it as the *lily grass,* and Grigson more recently suggested *Pride of the Thames.* My first sight of a Flowering Rush left me quite astonished. In amongst the Skull Cap and the Brookweed stood these tall and gorgeous sprays of pink - in a Downland fold! Like Rough Chervil, the flowers are on stalks of unequal length. Each umbel is on a leafless stalk, adding to the cleanness of it line. The rose pink of the petals is made complicated by the darkness of their veins. Frogbit, three prawn crackers, puts on winter buds which get buried in the relative warmth of the ditches' muddy bottom. There they lie dormant until spring. Additionally, in the autumn, it puts out seeds which fall through the water to reach the bottom: its insurance. In the

Flowering Rush

spring they germinate and rise to the surface as young plants.

Five-petalled Brookweed likes wet places near the sea. I have not seen it on the cliffs: certainly too dry - the coastal ditches here are an ideal habitat. It is a very characteristic looking plant as each flower stalk carries a tiny leaf-like bract alternating left and right along the stem.

Culpeper described a serious illness which overtook his son: "a raging disease called the bloody flux; the College of Physicians, not knowing what to make of it, called it the plague of the guts ... myself being in the county was sent for up; the only thing I gave him was Mallow bruised and boiled both in milk and drink: in two days (the blessing of God being upon it) cured him and I there, to

Brookweed

show my thankfulness to God, in communicating it to his creatures, leave it to posterity". Certainly, Marsh Mallow and the other mallows were put to endless medicinal uses. Herb-women toiled in the salt marshes of the Thames estuary to harvest root and leaf which were sold to the apothecaries in the capital. Its root was full of "clamie and slimie juice". A popular application was as a

Marsh Mallow

poultice or an ointment. It was appropriate to anything that might be inflammatory. "Kernels that rise behind the ears" - tuberculous neck glands - were rubbed with the ointment of Marsh Mallow. No longer turned to sweets, now left alone, wind-tossed in the salty reed beds or with the Hairy Buttercup in a drying ditch.

Greater Plantain

Greater Plantain tholes its endless trampling. By sympathy it was used to treat cuts and bruises. The North American Indians called it *white man's foot* as it followed his march across their plains. Anemophilous, and consequently ignored by bees. In France it was one of the important herbs of St John's Eve. Brought into the Christian fold it was *Christ's heel*. Van Dyck painted Plantain at the foot of the

Silverweed

Pineapple Weed

Crucifixion. Before that, for centuries its root was hung about the neck to ward tuberculosis off.

Before the introduction of the potato, *Silverweed* was cultivated in the Highlands and Islands for its root, which was both boiled and roasted. Otherwise it was a famine food, the root ground to meal for bread and porridge. In spring it can adorn and transform what was but a muddy gash in the winter hillside. Like Greater Plantain it minds not being crushed. Hence, it was stuffed into the shoes of the foot-weary traveller to ease his aches and pains. Trample the Pineapple Weed and its delicious scent gusts up. Its little flower heads are domed and at their base are pretty white-tipped bracts - it even looks a little bit like a pineapple.

At harvest time Hawthorn berries ripen and, it seems, quite suddenly the scrub is a smoky haze of red. The harvest is broadcast by white trumpets pushing skywards: the trumpets of a beauty, but a strangler too. Hedge Bindweed

Field Bindweed

Hedge Bindweed

twists only anticlockwise. *Devil's guts* to the gardener - roots like contorted entrails, *corn bind* or *bere bind* to the farmer - bere the barley whose stems it clambered on. The bell of its trumpet is a virginal white but from behind pink stripes are evident, as are two handsome large green bracts. The blooms close tight in wet and in the dark. They close, too, if you pick them. To keep them open, trailers can be immersed in water to prevent air from entering the stems. As for its beauty, to the Sussex peasant this funnel was nothing but a *piss pot*. But the Sussex peasantry was always obtuse - Stephen Blackmore, a shepherd who died in 1920, had only one arm. The other had been "taken clean off by a chaff-cutter" and when the doctors operated "my feather wouldn't allow 'em to give me no chloriform, not believin' in such stuff". In conversation, Sussex man is said to be slow of speech and, apparently, equally slow of thought: "a certain South

Wild Carrot

Downs man did not know either the correct pronunciation of his own name or that of the village in which he resided. On one occasion a person had been deputed to enquire after "Mr Pocock of Alciston" and meeting a man near the place in question asked if he could point out the residence of that individual. "Noa", was the reply: "never heered an him, an' doan't sick place". It turned out that the labourer was no other than Mr Pocock himself. "Why", said he, hearing of this later, "he should ha' axed fur "Mus Pack of Alison".

In the very centre of its umbel, the Wild Carrot has a small purple floret: a drop of blood spilled from the lace-maker's finger - St Anne, mother of the Virgin Mary, the patron saint of lace-makers. *Queen Anne's lace* is a general name for these carrotty umbellifers which grow happiest by the sea and on the chalk. This is their ideal world.

The *hardheads* bloom later than the more exotic relative, the Greater Knapweed. They flower on and on, past the time of Ploughman's Spikenard to the end-of-season Scabious. It is the most dominant plant of our seaside grassland in late summer. Knapweed species are quite limited in the United Kingdom but, like the Bramble, the genus, Centaurea, comprises several hundred species. Butterflies such as the Small Skipper, the commonest of the grassland skippers, the Marbled White, the Painted Lady and the rare Adonis Blue are drawn to its chaffie knops. Like the Daisy, it was used by country girls to foretell the course of love. With its florets taken off it was put inside the blouse and examined an hour later: if more florets had opened from the bud then love would come their way.

Painted Lady

Knapweed

Farewell summer says Solidago Virgaurea. It is also *Aaron's rod,* a name it shares with Mullein and Agrimony. A plant of dipping yellow racemes, one sees it here and there on roadside verges that run along the fringe of Downland - not a plant to climb the hill. It was a wound herb, a lotion for sores and ulcers in the mouth and throat. It caused Gerard to mull on human nature: "a dry herb from beyond the sea sold in London

Golden Rod

Duke of Argyll's Teaplant

Snowberry

for halfe a crowne an ounce. But since it was found in Hampstead wood ... no man will give halfe a crowne for a hundredweight of it: which plainely setteth forth our inconstancie and sudden mutabilitie, esteeming no longer of anything how precious soever it be than whilest it is strange and rare. This verifieth our English proverbe, far fetched and deare bought is best for ladies". He also talks of physicians harming more than they mend: plus ca change. Among the Soapwort and the Teasel great banks of Teaplant thrive in Tidemills dereliction, so too the Snowberry.

With Yarrow, Mugwort and Vervain, St John's Wort was one of the chief herbs of John the Baptist. His day is the 24th June. The Eve was the start of magic: fires would be lit to generate a purifying smoke that would endow the herbs with special powers: power to see off goblins and their like. Hold a leaf to the light and look through its translucent glands: the puncture marks of a wound herb,

Slender St John's Wort

substantiated by the bloodiness of its sap - the blood of St John. Hypericum perforatum was a strowing plant, strown not for freshness but to drive the Devil out. The Clusiaceae comprise worts with many variations of stem and leaf. Frequent in these parts are the Slender St John's Wort, the Square-stalked and the Trailing forms. These species synthesise several secondary compounds including tannins and essential oils. Its complex molecule, hypericin, has been attributed with an antidepressant effect and exhibits

Harebell

Pink

biological activity against retroviruses such as the Human Immunodeficiency Virus. It can also photosensitise the skin and has caused interactions with conventional medication: for example it can raise the blood concentration of anticonvulsant compounds, rendering them toxic.

Harebells are blowing in the hilltop breeze with Burnet Saxifrage, Betony and Pink. Not so frail as they might look: they range from the sand dunes to the high ground of our mountains. Refined in every aspect of design - a shapely clapper in its bell, its pale blue stigma. Later it forms a beehive capsule which dispenses seed through perforations at the base. Unhappily, its sites are few in this stretch of Downs - I

Harebell

Nettle-leaved Bellflower

Hedge Bindweed

Frogbit

can think of only a handful of places where it grows and only in small numbers. It was not to be picked: *witch's thimbles, gowk's thimbles (Scots - fool's thimbles), old man's bell, cuckoo's thimble*. Cuckoos, hares, witches and devils: all hocus-pocus, but subversive to the Church and so it was christened *Our Lady's thimble*.

More than fifty summers have gone cold since my friend Dennis first saw the Pink near Firle. All our Dianthus species - Maiden, Deptford and Cheddar - are rare and how this small colony arose is quite unclear. Why it has neither extended nor shrunk away in half a century is equally unclear. Other "bell-floures", as Gerard called them, are found on Caburn's slopes - these blue 'foxgloves' push with Agrimony through leggy colour-leached grasses. Just outside a copse they are brushed gently by the capricious fronds of a dancing Ash. The white style, an uvula emerging from the flower's throat, was its signature. Additionally, it secretes a yellow latex: no clearer cipher for the pus that clings to inflammed tonsils - hence *throatwort* or *uvulawort*. The Nettle-leaved Bellflower was called Canterbury Bell by early botanists as it grew freely in the woods near Canterbury.

Pheasant's-eye

Like some orchids Pheasant's-eye may lie dormant for many years then emerge in a startling show. Not for some years now. However, it does grow in small numbers in meadow and in beechwood.

Two cliff-top rarities are now in flower, Wall Germander with its leaves like molten wax, finely crimped about the edges, and the carrot that is luminous by the light of the moon. A small colony at Cuckmere Haven is the only wild colony of Wall Germander in Sussex. Sunk in rabbit scrapes, it creeps into the wind-clipped grasses of the shortest turf. But wait till dark arrives - travel by moonlight, a silver dance on the darkened Channel, to see Moon Carrot glow at night. There are two extensive sites between Eastbourne and Lewes and otherwise a handful of sites in Bedfordshire and Cambridgeshire. It

Wall Germander

is recorded that there is a single plant in Hertfordshire.

Shetlanders call it *dead man's mittens* - half-open buds are like livid fingernails poking through the ground. Felwort, the autumn gentian, is a plant of the well-drained chalk. Elsewhere it is seen in limestone soils and dune-slacks. Sub-species are confined to the limestone dunes of the Hebrides, Orkneys, Shetlands and Northern Scotland. Here amongst the Eyebright and Squinancywort, the Bell Heather and the Scabious, it is a short turf plant. Despite its many heads it is not showy: perhaps disappointingly drab for a Gentian. Culpeper was aware of two native Gentians, Gentianella amarella and Gentianella campestris at a time when the Gentian was imported from abroad for medicinal and veterinary use. "When kine are bitten on the udder by venomous beasts" Gentian was applied.

Moon Carrot

Felwort

Thistledown

Thistledown was gathered by the poor to stuff their pillows when feathers were running short. Gerard was indignant over the rich upholsterers who adulterated their feather stuffs with down: "a deceit" which "would be looked into"! The thistle root was the poor man's supper: but always a better medicine than it was a meal. This, another chalk thistle, sometimes known as the *picnic thistle:* the jellyfish of the Downs, a hidden stinger.

Dwarf Thistle

Catkins showed early on the Hazel, which is now early with its nuts - ready for picking. Coppiced Hazel with its fine, straight growth is used in hurdle making, fencing and in the construction of wattle and daub walls. The time to harvesting has shortened in recent decades through the effects of climate change. The Downs are coming into fruit with crab apples, elderberries, sloes and blackberries - with Hazelnuts the making of a topnotch hedgerow jam. In the shadow of the Hazel, where the Early Purple grew, stands

Hazelnuts

Nipplewort. By sympathy it was a healer of "women's sore breasts, as well as their nipples when they are ulcerated" [C]: the ailments of the nursing mother. Like Vervain, its flowers hang in space like a floral planetarium. Wall Lettuce is another plant of woodland banks; it grows tall and gangly

Sloe berries and Traveller's Joy

Elderberries

Nipplewort

Deadly Nightshade berries

in Friston Forest, a yellow candelabra in the beechwood gloaming.

The glaucous leaf rosettes of Yellow-wort have peppered Downland since the early days of spring. Now, as an afterthought of summer, they bloom. A chalky plant, on open tops, steep declines, gentle contours, and liking light and dryness. Gerard saw it on the "chalkie cliffes of Greenhive in Kent". To the early botanists it was the *yellow centaury*. While the flowerhead is reminiscent of Centaury the habit of the plant is quite dissimilar. The species name, perfoliata, refers to the piercing of the conjoined leaves by its stem. This is the wild gentian of the chalk.

Late summer berries and vanilla-scented flowers drape the scrub. Not yet an old man, nor yet bearded, it scrambles, twines and ramps. In some places Traveller's Joy forms impenetrable tangles, for which it was known as a choker, a witch's plant - *hag rope*. A flower without true petals, its little stars are coloured sepals. Droplets of nectar form on its filaments not from conventional nectaries. Such a climber that it will cap a tree or shrub

Yellow-wort

Centaury

as high as fifty feet. The *Devil's guts* and *witche's rope* was inevitably exorcised and the throttler, at a pen-stroke, was the *Virgin's bower.* Gerard named it "Traveller's Joy" and "esteemed it only for pleasure", but country folk had it for a baccy: *smoking cane, shepherd's delight, boy's bacca*

Yellow-wort

Wall Lettuce

and *poor man's friend* - it burns poorly on a fire. In winter its stems hang, liana-like, in the naked woods, some as thick as a wrestler's thigh.

Each orb of Dodder's blossom feeds from a red, tangled umbilical cord it hangs about its victim. It seems that blood is passing from one to the other. But this is fanciful, Dodder is not sinister - more like a string of little pink lamps draped carelessly on a Christmas tree. Hard to find hereabouts and on Knapweed not Gorse or Heather.

In twilight, even better by moonlight, late summer is the time to experience the headiest of scents. A love-plant whose leaves, not blossoms, are significant of felicity - in opposite pairs and of a twining habit. Pepys said "its trumpet blows scent, not sound". Honeysuckle is one of the earliest leaves to burst, often in December. It clasps and coils opposite ways to Bindwind, with such an iron grip as to constrict supporting stems into a barley twist. Visited by long-tongued moths, it is also a creche for the eggs of the Comma and the White Admiral. The Convolvulus Hawk Moth, banded on its back, with the longest wing span of any of our insects, visits to drink its nectar in the safety of the dark. The Hummingbird Hawk Moth, a summer visitor from France, visits Honeysuckle not by night but in the daylight. Its wing beat is so rapid as to make its wings invisible as it hovers at the font.

Dodder

Honeysuckle

..... and ever the Yaffle

Traveller's Joy and Honeysuckle

September

From a brow the traveller is beckoned by distant, disappearing tracks - etched white but fading into the far blue-grey. They call you to the west for Rampions, east for Autumn Lady's-tresses, north for shimmering banks of Scabious or south for Lavender. As summer ebbs, strange White Orchids fill their frilly trumpets with green nectar.

Autumn Lady's-tresses

Autumn Lady's-tresses grow shyly on bostal banks where Kidney Vetch and Rockrose are all but done. Here the Adonis Blue flits and sips. Plant numbers vary year on year - this may have something to do with the behaviour of the fungus which infects its roots. Orchid seed needs to be infected by a mycorrhizal fungus to ensure the orchid's growth and many orchids subsequently maintain a close relationship with the fungus. The main food plant of the Adonis Blue is the Horseshoe Vetch, which flowered earlier on the same dry slopes. Plant colours elicit different behavioural responses from butterflies according to the time of day: a given species may respond to yellow in the morning and, at midday, switch to red. Male and female Adonis have a chequered wing edge and their caterpillar is striped yellow. Confined to the chalk, this electric blue butterfly is specific to the plants and climate

Adonis Blue

of our Downland. Its caterpillars are carried off by ants and taken to their nest, there safe from predators. The caterpillars "sing" to the ants to pacify them and also produce a sugar liquid, the ants' reward.

Huge colonies of Scabious have turned the hillsides blue, an evanescent even an illusory blue: the blue is only apparent from close to - wade through a sea of heads, glance back and they have 'gone'. At the end of summer's script, Devil's Bit, comes from a short, thick, blackish root: "this root was longer until", as the friars say, "the Devil bit away the rest of it for spite, envying its usefulness to mankind" [C]. Marsus Diaboli was its Medieval Latin name, hence "Devil's bite". Despite the curtailment of its power the apothecaries used it widely - against the plague, fevers, venomous bites, as a gargle against the swelling of the "almonds" (tonsils), as a poultice to take away bruises and as a wormicide. Its ovary drips nectar - an autumnal food source for bees

Devil's Bit Scabious

Devil's Bit with Small Scabious

and butterflies. Most beekeepers "close" their hives by September but I like to keep my bees at work, hoping for an extension of the summer's warmth. Small Tortoiseshells jig contentedly among the purple anthers.

The horns of the Yellow Poppy are cracking open to release their seed,

Small Tortoiseshell

having got to impressive lengths, sometimes as long as 40 cm. The beaked fruits of the Sea Radish are about to discharge their cargo to the tide, while Sea Aster and Sea Purslane shade the salt marsh with gentle frosted tints. The mauve and yellow of the Aster

Sea Purslane

Sea Aster

Yellow Horned Poppy seed pods

harmonises with the Purslane's grey-green sheen: the sheen from a layer of papery scales which clad the leaf and stop it drying out. Before the arrival of the Michaelmas Daisies from the New World (17th century) the Sea Aster was a popular Elizabethan garden plant. It was widely used against childhood illnesses, notably the squinancy and the falling sickness.

Sea Radish pods

Autumn colours on the shoreline, too: the Samphire flowers are browning over but Toadflax is yet to set its seed. Formerly a well known weed in flax - useless - therefore 'toad'. Now a yellow flame in stubble. 'Urinalis' to the apothecaries, its yellow marking it a

Toadflax

diuretic. Its narrow leaves spiral up the stem to the *squeeze jaw:* it takes a heavy insect to prise its maw apart. Grasses now are pale, bleached to tan and straw. Early summer's colours all washed out emphasise the whiteness of the Hogweed and the Carrot. Some Carline Thistles are still in flower, others are taking on their dessicated winter look. Gromwell's stone soon to tumble. Tracts of Wild Carrot and Kidney Vetch still send colour rushing down the slopes and into coombes, whilst great swarms of Daddy-longlegs are blown across the grassland. The fruits of Agrimony and of Dropwort are now on show, and worth a close inspection. The dainty rundles of Bristly Oxtongue sit amongst its flowers - a particularly dainty clock, its workings as fine as gossamer. Hedgerows turned to larders, now full of ripening fruit, plumed seeds bursting from their capsules. Black Medick is no longer hard to tell from Hop Trefoil now the flesh has fallen. The Crab is ready to be dunted - fruit in the hedge brings up an atavistic urge - time for making jams

Gromwell seed

and tarts. "Crab" from its quirky fruit, not quite right and hard. With wheat and barley cut we can inspect the treasures in the stubble. Good corn weeds are becoming rarer but there are still many species worth searching out. Fluellen's flowers reach up, periscopic, craning for a view. The Round-leaved and Sharp-leaved species are both quite hairy, the Sharp-leaved just like halberds with a chocolate coloured lip. Nearby Lilac fancies protrude from a long, chamfered calix tube - but a beauty in decline. When the long capsule splits pale brown shiny oval seeds emerge, like highly polished mirrors - these are *Venus' looking glasses.*

It goes under *monkey's face* in Sussex. Elsewhere it is a *kiss-me* or *love-in-vain* plant: the large lower petal is the

Wild Carrot

Kidney Vetch

Bristly Oxtongue

Dropwort in seed

Viola Tricolor

girl and the petal on either side her suitors: one destined to love in vain. Oberon squeezed its juice into Titania's eyes so that she would fall in love with fatuous Bottom.

Pansy came into use in England around 1500 and derives from the French pensée, a thought. Milton's "pansy freak'd with jet" refers to dark petal lines which converge to lead the long-tongued insects to a pool of nectar. The textured petals of Viola Tricolor come in yellow, blue or pink, hence the herb of the Blessed Trinity. The Field Pansy is smaller-flowered and has its sepals poking past its petals.

Known for the *black spotte* on its leaf, left by the *Devil's pinch,* pulled, taken to be useless and discarded. Later Persicaria became a dye plant.

Seemingly inured to herbicides are Black Nightshade and Sun Spurge. Nightshade's berries, like the Privet's, go from green to black, a black which spills onto stem and leaf. The toxicity of Black Nightshade varies

Black Medick seed

amongst its populations, some plants are edible and some are deadly. Humans can develop tolerance with repeat exposure to solanine - vindication for Mithradates - otherwise solanine produces drowsiness and ultimately paralysis. The Rappahannock Indians used leaves of the related American Black Nightshade to make a narcotic tea.

Now the thistle seed is set. Buoyed up by the unseen currents its down will bounce and tumble, spewing out in endless streams, while *wild clematis* cascades down hillsides, like a mountain burn in spate. Though the Creeping Thistle is one of the worst weeds for the farmer, it is a granary for the Goldfinch which

Field Pansy

Black Nightshade

Honeysuckle and Bramble

Agrimony fruits

Fluellen

Redshank

Venus's Looking-glass

Hop Trefoil

Creeping
Thistle

Sun
Spurge

Willowherb

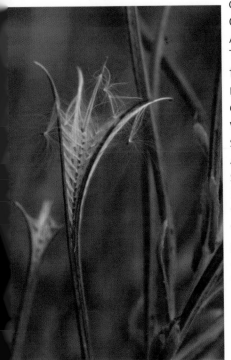

congregates in large flocks to swoop excitedly where the thistles grow. There is now less grazing on the Downs and rather more arable than there was in the 18th century. Ploughing on the Downs during World War II to increase food production reduced the number of sheep flocks considerably. In 1788, between Eastbourne and Steyning, a 33 mile tract of Downland held some 200,000 ewes. The Southdown breed we know today was developed from a small native heath sheep. John Ellman developed a breed good for wool, which lambed early and was hardy. The characteristic short, thick wool, the shortest among the British sheep covers most of the face as well as coming down to the hocks. The carcass is of a fairly high quality and fetched good prices. Such enormous numbers of sheep were important in keeping down the scrub and close grazing was advantageous to small wild herbs. Generations of such grazing has resulted in a great richness of Downland flowers in those places where ancient turf survives.

Between the two World Wars the seasonal rhythm of the Downland shepherds' lives would have differed little from that of their distant forerunners. At summer's end, as now, the ewes ran on the Thyme-scented grass by day and at night were folded on mustard or clover leys. Later in the year red-raddled rams were turned on the ewes, usually one ram to fifty. By February the pregnant ewes were kept enclosed and fed on turnips when the shepherd would be busy building his lambing yard. An important rural economy formed around the sheep, including the coppicing of Chestnut and Hazel for the construction of sheep hurdles. In April the sheep and their lambs would be folded on winter cereals such as rye, oats and barley. As the spring grass grew the ewes would be let out for half days and by June the lambs would be weaned to a glorious ley of pink-striped Sainfoin.

..... and ever the Yaffle

October

The track that rises through the stubble field is more than just a score across the Downs: it is a sepia-coloured memory from summer's brightness. My journey through rippling chest-high barley, yet another item of memory stamped upon the landscape - each human journey recorded, laid down with the track's increasing definition.

Wild Mignonette blooms on. This is a typical habitat: a path side where there are bare patches in the turf from winter ground disturbance. On sunlit days, even now, this prime nectar plant will be visited by foraging bees. Another source of nectar for late-flying butterflies and moths is Ivy - the last important honey plant of the year. It yields an unpalatable honey but it is important for colonies struggling to build their stores against winter's famine. A large colony may need upwards of 40 lbs of honey to see it through a hard winter. As lower temperatures make it harder for bees to concentrate their nectar it is fortunate that Ivy nectar is unusually concentrated - unless the water content is adequately reduced, stored honey would ferment in the comb. Ivy, so generous with

Ivy

Scentless Mayweed

Bramble

its nectar that it may run freely from the flowers - like honeydew on the Lime. Like the Holly it is a caterpillar food plant for the Brimstone. Its berries ripen at the winter solstice and make a good larder for the birds. In the shelter of its leaves the adult Brimstone over-winters. As early as January, as long as there is some warmth, it will be the first butterfly to take wing. In April the sulphur yellows will dance across Ground Ivy's purple carpet. Another butterfly, one of hedgerows and woodland clearings, the Holly Blue, has an unusual relation with the Ivy. It alternates its caterpillar food plants - the first generation caterpillars in May and June feed from the Holly bud and the second generation in August feed from Ivy. Like the Holly, the Ivy was apotropaic: both protectors through the dark cold of winter. In pre-Christian times so strong was this belief these woods were incorporated into boats and buildings. The Vikings built Rowan wood into their ships - Ran, the Norse sea-goddess,

Field Woundwort

Fumitory

Henbit Dead-nettle

rarely wrecked ships with Rowan in their structure.

In the stubble, the Scentless Mayweed is still in flower. Its relative, Stinking Mayweed, was a serious problem to the harvesters in centuries gone by. Blistering of the skin was severe enough to put men off work. Few brambles now.

Overshadowed by the brightness of the Toadflax, some delicate dead-nettles and a dainty Woundwort. A pretty pouting lip hangs from Henbit Dead-nettle's elongated trumpet.

A 12th century herbal had it that Fumitory was "engendered of a coarse fumosity rising from the earth" - its juice, as with smoke, made the eyes water.

Clouded Yellow

Nettle

In the United States it is called *fume-root* - the pulling of the root gives off an acrid smell, supposedly like nitric acid. Its fine feathery leaves piled on the ground are said to look like smoke seeping from the earth: more smoke. (Sit and watch a nettle. You will see it put out little puffs of smoke). The flower colouring is unusual - looking as if the petal tips were dipped in purple dye. It has the distinction of producing a nectar disdained by insects. Despite the drop in temperature Clouded Yellows are still quite active. Nights lengthen. The herbs spend longer out of light. Moon Carrot, the Prince of night now gone, no amber petals nor Painted Ladies to be caught in the lighthouse's winking beam. The plants' retraction, their retreat to earth, begins as winds get keener and rain is driven rather than arriving softly. Yet Yarrow, caught in starlight, still flowers through the dark.

The Red Dead-nettle and the Black Bindwind are two of the commonest arable weeds. Better the *bee-nettle,* I think - it is a very early source of nectar at the beginning of the year. Rustics and their pigs used it as a winter green in times past: it can flower right through winter in these milder climes.

Small Toadflax

Red Dead-nettle

Fool's Parsley

Worth searching for is the Small Toadflax. This little gaping one differs from true toadflaxes as its petal tube is not fully closed by the fold of the lower lip. Beside it you will very likely find a post-script to the harvest - Fool's Parsley. Gerard noted its "naughtie smell". Its leaf bears a passing likeness to parsley,

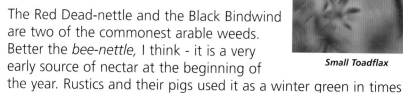
Corn Spurrey

Wall Speedwell

Buxbaum's Speedwell

Yew

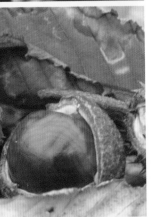

Bramble flower

the pot herb, but this is a poisonous plant laced with coniine and cynopine. Like the Wild Carrot it has attractive bracts. Culpeper saw that hares were fond of parsley and a good way to decoy a hare was to sow a spot of ground with parsley. Wall Speedwell and Buxbaum's Speedwell add their pretty blues to the cornfield pot pourri. But one weed of Downland fields, Corn Spurrey, is grown elsewhere as a fodder crop, and there is archaeological evidence that it was an Iron Age crop, likely ground to meal. The Privet berries have now gone black, Rampion blooms on late, as do some clumps of Marjoram and Basil. Ash leaves yellow, Chestnuts brown as days shorten and a chill seeps into lengthening Downland nights. The dark and cold kill chlorphyll but leave the other pigments - carotene for yellow and anthocyanin for red. Dry, sunny days and cold nights intensify the reds and yellows. The Yew keeps its colour. Happily, it extends beyond the churchyard to the scrub. The only non-poisonous part of the yew is the fleshy aril round the seed. Taxol, which is important in the treatment of ovarian cancer, is derived from yew. Originally it was taken from the bark of the Pacific Yew but such were the demands upon the species that it neared extinction. More recently taxol has come from needle clippings from our native Yew. In Sussex its berries are known as *"snottygogs"*. Robert Turner, 1664, wrote that the Yew is put in churchyards "to attract and imbibe putrefaction and gross oleaginous vapours exhaled out of the graves". Henbane's seed box is a dainty caddy with a flip top - to be well shaken on the cliff-top by winter storms in store.

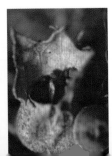

..... and ever the Yaffle

November

Inky blue-grey skies lour over Downland. Its grasses are covered in day-long dew. Tracks darken, shortened by the autumn mists. That sense of infinity they offered up - like unravelled string - has gone. Old Man's Beard hangs like smoke around the scrub and Hawthorn berries darken. A valley away a plume of smoke lifts indolently - the scrub burners are at work, their fire a pin point of  red, just visible. Hawthorn scrogs, tiny winter silhouettes, march along a far off ridge. Though the sun is vapid and the landscape going to sepia, the scrub is rich with colour: palest is the Elder, somewhat darker the Wayfaring Tree, browns from Privet, the reddy hue of Hawthorn and the near black of Sloe. These scrub mosaics are best appreciated viewed from a lofty spot when the sun comes out. Branches may be bare of leaves, but the gall is on the rose and Jew's-

Robin's Pincushion

ear on the Elder. Jew's-ear is a downward-facing bracket fungus, shaped just like a human ear, mainly associated with the Elder on which Judas met his end. In the spring shepherds of earlier times used Elder to make the teats for their weak lambs' feeding bottles - the pith removed, bound round with rags and fitted to a wine or spirit bottle. King Alfred's cakes - *crampballs* - often grow on fallen timber and in the grassland the puffballs swell. Diced up and dried, Puffball burns well in a bee smoker. Even now the Mayweed and the Mugwort have not gone over, and you may happen upon a crowd of Nodding Thistles still dressed bright in purple-pink. Cowslip pods still hold some seed, as do the capsules of the Spotted Orchid. The orchid seed is brown and rod-like if shaken onto paper for inspection - like bacilli through a lens. The capsule of the Spotted Orchid is slashed along its length like an Elizabethan sleeve. Now, near the dead of year, few flowers in the turf, though an odd sprig of Thyme can still be seen, and Wall Rocket's Channel watch. Honeybees are quiet in their hive. The mass of pollen and nectar gathered by the insects over the spring and summer months is hard to comprehend. A colony of honeybees will need some 90 lbs of honey through the year - importantly a store to over-winter on, this means the foraging bees have to collect almost 500 lbs of nectar. As to pollen, a colony needs more than 60 lbs - think of the effort - a hazel catkin holds more than 4 million pollen spores - each grain is virtually weightless. The efforts of the walker, too, are well rewarded - baked and dry in summer, the turf had lost its spring but now it holds more water it is elastic and is at its best for walking on.

Wild Thyme

Cowslip seed pods

Annual Wall Rocket

..... and ever the Yaffle

December

On a still December night, no wind, no calling bird, just a bat by starlight on the track that carries me due east. Dropped halfway off the hill crest, my path runs parallel to the valley floor below me on my right. Above, to my left the summit runs, a sharp black edge against a blue-grey sky. On it, hung low, the Plough. As I progress so it moves too across the Downs, dipping and rising with each step I take, its share turning a single long black furrow. Phekda and Merak, on its cutting edge, glance off sleeping orchids and the stumpy roots of scabious. Briefly, a brighter star, not scintillating, is assimilated by the Plough: now they are eight. Its programmed flash and its too rapid movement brand it interloper, not locked into far-awayness: soon it will come to earth, cool and darken. The white track falls towards the valley floor and turns south towards the cliffs. The Plough is gone and the sky ink-pink.

Sloe Berries

Black Bryony berries

"When Gorse is out of bloom, kissing is out of season": Gorse always puts out a flush of flower just before the winter solstice. It is the ideal base for a Christmas garland of Downland fruits and flowers, though not the easiest material to work with. Its stunning yellow looks so well by the black berries of Privet, the bright red berries of Black Bryony and the orange fruits of Stinking Iris. Hard to believe that all these gay colours have come from the winter scrub. As a token of fidelity a spray of Gorse should be included in the bouquet of a country bride. Surprisingly, Gorse is rare in Sweden. At his first sight of English Gorse Linnaeus, overcome, fell to his knees and wept. Known in the West Country as furze and in

Gladdon

Old Man's Beard

Scotland as whin, its local Sussex name is hawth. Like Heather, which grows in similar situations, it was once valuable in the rural economy: as a fuel, a fodder, a dye plant and a thatch. Before the general availability of coal, Gorse was burned as a fuel for brick and lime kilns. Its spines were crushed in West Country cider presses to make it a manageable fodder. Indeed, farmers harvested it, cutting it every third year. Upper shoots, which are softest, well-bruised were fed to dairy cattle. Goats can eat its spines, and on Lullington Heath a herd has been introduced to keep gorse down. Its yellow was taken against the jaundice and its flowers were turned to wine. A good

sized piece tied to a rope and hauled up and down made an effective chimney brush.

The brown capsule of the *Gladdon* splits - an orange star is formed by the neatly ordered berries which will shine all winter long - unexpected points of colour in the shin-high privet. Some dark

Ant igloos

cold months yet till the Early Purple Orchids put more colour in this scrub. Strange that the Old Man's Beard is still intact: winds that have whipped across the scrub should have torn the plumes off long since, winds with the force to sculpt stiff Hawthorns - branches turned to a girl's tousled hair, streaming in the wind.

In recent winters snow has rarely been seen lying on the Downs. Then, muffled white, the hills and denes assume an absolute tranquility. Dark and leafless trees stand stark, hawthorns are stuffed white, but not with blossom. Ants are in their igloos.

Most people crave light and colour in the depths of winter, and bright skies, bright berries and the sight of sun will lift the spirits. But wait for nightfall to see winter Downland at its best: shadowy thickets, trees in silhouette, moon-shadows, the sweep of a dark hillside against a star-laden sky and a pale chalk track snaking into darkness. If the wind is high, so much the better, trees and shrubs are agitated into their own queer

Spindle Wood

Burnet Rose hips

music. No leaf sounds, only the percussion of bare branches. So provoked, each tree emits a novel repertoire of sounds - the timbre of the notes dictated by the size and the hardness of the branches and the force of their collisions. The Blackthorn emits high-pitched squeaks and scrapes. The Sycamore is stiffer and even a forceful wind struggles to extract some notes. It is the Ash which is most musical of all - its bare skeleton flexes keenly, clacks and clatters. All quite different, of course, if trees are jammed close together and their branches rattle on each other. Hawthorns squeak and creak from the rubbing of their close-placed trunks. In a wind-tormented copse, the moon above, the long-sustained chord you hear is the whistle of the wind itself.

Ash and Hazel, Sloe and Spindle, a hedgerow canopy banked up with snow - under which the Ramsons sleep. Jackdaws raid the Holm Oak though most acorn cups are empty now.

Snow redefines the landscape: what was inconspicuous now draws the eye, a bank of Ash becomes a tangent, Sloe's thorn gets blacker still. Under the snow a vivid green: Spring in the heart of winter - Alexanders grow through the winter and bring a taste of myrrh. Myrrh is harvested as a gum-resin from the Commiphora shrub in its native Somalia and Ethiopia. In the Near East it is used, rather like propolis, as an antiseptic mouthwash as well as a perfume. Egyptians used it as an embalming agent (kyphi). Whether or not Alexanders really taste of myrrh, it can be used as a pot herb. The roots are a poor man's parsnip, its leaves and stems softened in butter are eaten like asparagus. But better in the winter moonlight, than in a pot, when their leaves shine silver where badgers pass and foxes howl.

Sloe, hybridized with the Cherry Plum, is the forerunner of the Damson. Known to the Sussex

peasant as *winter picks,* it had its uses:- "it is the juice of this berry that makes the famous marking ink to write upon linen, it being so strong and acid, that no other acid known will discharge it" [C], and still is used as a flavouring for gin.

Surprising hedgebank colours from the Spindle and the Dogwood - the Italians refer to spindle as the *priest's biretta,* a cardinal's bonnet gone shocking pink. The gaping capsule reveals a shining orange fruit. William Turner claimed it from the Dutch who used its wood for making spindles. Gypsies camping in the old chalk pits made skewers from its hard white wood, hence *skewerwood.* Alternatively *louse-berry* - the fruits were baked to a dry powder which was then rubbed in hair against nits and lice. In a good year some boughs are so heavy with fruit as to give the impression of pink bees hanging in a cluster. *Gatter-tree* is yet another of its names and a name it shares with Dogwood. Useless fruits hang on summer Dogwood, called by John Parkinson the *dog berry tree* because the berries are "not fit to be eaten or given to a dogge". But its wood, clad in a foetid bark, was useful, hard as iron, made into wedges for splitting softer woods. Fit, too, for a pestle. It was valued by the Greeks for its hardness, robust enough for javelins and spearheads. Indeed, myth has it that the Trojan Horse was built of Dogwood. On the domestic front the twigs, if chewed, will separate into a primitive toothbrush. Although it makes its home on chalk and limestone its red stems are not so common in these parts. But, come May when some heat is back, the green Hairstreak will seek it out.

Dogwood and Spindle Berries

..... *and ever the* ℐaffle

Black Bryony Berries

January

Redundant seed heads, rimy and brightly lit, can match the beauty of long gone flowers. The moonlit Hawthorn casts its blue shadow on the snow. Winter Heliotrope, the first wild flower of the year, blankets roadside verges, often by the village sign-post, runs in and out of ditches dank and piled with oak leaves. It was brought to England in the 19th century from the Mediterranean and it proved to be a choker, but take a few tufted heads indoors and they will fill your room with the scent of marzipan.

Strangely, as a wild plant, the Snowdrop is almost absent from Ireland and there is debate over its native status here. It was cultivated in the 16th century but was not recorded from the wild until the end of the 18th century. Its distribution around churches and early pagan sites of worship suggested that it could be an introduction. *Fair maids* in some counties, in Sussex it was *death's flower* - another of the plants best left outside; risk a death by bringing it indoors. Better as, *snow-piercer*, a gallant winter plant. Each drooping head has three white sepals and three shorter green-tipped petals, holding a secret well of nectar secreted for early flying bees. The apothecaries used the Snowdrop against tuberculosis, indeed Culpeper used it to treat his own daughter's illness. She had tuberculous neck glands from which he "drew out one quarter of a pint of corruption" - cheesy pus. The nectaries, the nectar yielding glands, can be situated in almost any part of a plant - the sepal, the stamen, the ovary - but quite unusually the snowdrop secretes its syrup from grooves on the inner surface of its petal. In 1899 Keble Martin, then 23 years old, made the first drawing for "The Concise British Flora" - the Snowdrop. The first

Teasel

Winter Heliotrope

Snowdrop

Periwinkle

Winter Aconite

Spurge Laurel

and last illustration incorporating leaves of a different plant to that being featured (it would be some 66 years before his work was complete and his epic work published).

Still with Culpeper: on the Lesser Periwinkle "leaves eaten by man and wife together cause love between them". Earlier venereal concoctions included powdered earthworm - a last resort. It flowers in woodland with Spurge Laurel and Dog's Mercury. Like the *cuckoo-pint* and the Early Purple Orchid a plant of fertility, also a symbol of immortality - perhaps through being evergreen. Paradoxically in Italy it was a death flower - a periwinkle flower was put on the heads of the condemned, awaiting execution. More mundanely, *cut-finger,* a plant for stemming blood. You may find it in the churchyard with the Winter Aconite: unlike the *snow-piercer* the Aconite will only open in temperatures above 10°C. A pretty little alien, too timid to extend beyond the graveyard wall.

Light floods through stands of Ash and Beech while their leafy canopy is off, so Violets, Privet, Periwinkle, Ivy, beech bark and the unfurling of green *cuckoo-pint,* are all lit bright. Spurge Laurel takes advantage of the light and blossoms now before it is put in summer shadow. Early flying lepidoptera and bumblebees come to the scent of its greenish flowers. Its trumpets hang in clusters, on better days spot-lit by a shaft of sun. Here, in the shelter of the woods, it is at the northern limit of its range. It manufactures poisons at which the birds can safely peck.

No redder berry than the Cotoneaster's. Any track that is deeply cut in chalk will be splashed in its red through winter. The Wild Cotoneaster is very rare indeed, confined to the limestone of Great Ormes Head in northern Wales. The Small-leafed

Cotoneaster is a native of the Himalayas and was introduced to Britain in 1824. It likes chalk or limestone and preferably near the sea. The Himalayan Cotoneaster has orange coloured, egg-shaped fruits.

Small-leaved Cotoneaster

From the windswept chalk look to the ordered patchwork, the outside of Downland - too constrained, no rise and fall to give it rhythm, no romance of disappearing tracks, no secret coombes where orchids grow unseen - turn back and take the chalk.

..... and ever the Yaffle

Spurge Laurel blossom under snow

February

This tracks connects with that, each with the other, into a mesh, like some queer and giant web spun by a spideroid across the Downs. A chaotic web; each strand in it unique, with its own length and gradient, its surface like a fingerprint and each bounded by its own community of plants. Thrift, Horned Poppy and Sea Beet all keep attractive leaves through winter. Tiny buds on Blackthorn now, and the Privet leaf is breaking. The glaucous colour of the Poppy's foliage is due to a layer of waxy substance which reduces water loss. Sea Beet, a member of the Goosefoot family, has an enormous tap root which helps it withstand drought, cliff falls leave it dangling in the wind. A wintrier presence is the skeleton of Burdock, gallows fallen into disrepair. Handsome

Yellow Horned Poppy

Sea Beet root

Dog's Mercury

vaulted Ash creates cathedrals full of light, their floors greened over with Dog's Mercury, indicator of an ancient woodland. Its fresh growth surrounds the mossed-over remains of a Clematis rope, but for best effect see it pushing through Horse Chestnut litter, which still holds its rusty pigment. Dioecious, poisonous, useless: a dog plant. Each part of it is poisonous: dangerously emetic, purgative, narcotic. Throughout the country it is a plant of snakes and goblins: in Sussex *snake's victuals*. It fruits are quirky, too: bi-lobed with a fuzzy coat.

Usually white, sometimes purple, pink or mauve, Sweet Violet is the only richly scented violet. The strange thing is that its scent is lost as soon as it is sensed. With its perfume the plant produces ionine which immediately kills the sense of smell. Snow comes stealthily to cover it and lock away the scent. Unusual in

Sweet Violet

Dog's Mercury

that it has no stems: the flowers hang on leafless stalks that come directly from the leaf rosette. Its neatly scalloped leaves enlarge prodigiously once the seed is set. In some species self-pollination is a second option once cross-pollination has failed; in others such as barley, self-pollination takes place as soon as the flower is open and cross-pollination never occurs naturally. The most extreme form of self-pollination occurs in cleistogamous flowers where the flower never opens properly: Sweet Violets produce both open and cleistogamous flowers. The young spring plants are quite rich in vitamin C and safe then as a salad leaf, but as the plant ages it accumulates poisonous protoanemonine, found in several of the Ranunculacae. The High Brown Fritillary, a scrubland butterfly, lays its eggs on violet leaves and will feed off the Bramble flower at mid-summer. The largest British fritillary, the Silver-washed, is on the wing in later summer - it chooses to lay its eggs on tree bark, but near to Violets.

Coltsfoot

Son afore the father - flower before the leaf - is one of Coltsfoot's Scottish names. Mother called it 'tishilago', a corruption of 'tussilago', its generic name. A plant to smoke: another *poor man's baccy.* It was smoked for health: used against a cough, (tussis L, cough) hence *cough-wort.* When the leaves first unfold they are covered in fine down which duly disappears from the upper surface. It was from the leaf's undersurface that the down was collected and made into tinder: "wrapped in a rag, and boyl'd a little in Lee, adding a little Salt-Petre and after dried in the sun" (John Pechey, 1694). The bent stalks of the plant in bud suggest a shepherd's crook till they straighten as the flowers open. Its leaf is hoof-shaped and is otherwise known as *bull-foot, calf's-foot, ass's foot, horse-hoof, sow-foot* and *foal-foot.*

"If you dig up the root of Lesser Celandine you shall perceive the exact image of the disease which they commonly call the piles": a herb to ease their pain and swelling, and stop their bleeding. The roots were taken inwardly and an ointment made of their leaves. Two common forms of the plant occur and are distinguished once flowering is over. Those with little white bulbils where the leaf stalk

Lesser Celandine

joins the stem are found as garden weeds. If without bulbils it is the Celandine native of our woodlands. Its flowers are "thrum" or "pin". Its cousin, Greater Celandine, encourages the ants to spread its seeds - each has a fleshy protrusion, an aril, rich in oils, an inducement for the portage.

It is the time when Gilbert White's idiot-boy was coming back to life after his winter torpor - like the bees he loved - "in the winter he dozed away his time within his father's house by the fireside in a kind of torpid state, seldom departing from the chimney-corner but in the summer he was all alert and in quest of his game in the fields and on sunny banks. Honeybees, Bumblebees and Wasps were his prey. He had no apprehensions from their stings but would seize them with his bare hands and at once disarm them of their weapons and suck their bodies for the sake of their honey bags". They were his sole object. Now the beehive puts out scouts to seek for forage after the drag of months with activity suspended. Now is the time to get the queen to lay.

..... *and ever the* *Yaffle*

March

There is no flower quite like Moschatel: a solitary species in a family all of its own. A tiny pale green beauty with five flowers in a unique assemblage: the *town-hall clock*. Its cuboidal head has a flower on each side and one on top. Its newly broken leaves might be overlooked as the Wood Anemone save that comes slightly later. Its scent of musk, or almond, or even elderblossom, strengthens towards dusk and it is stronger still when dew has fallen. There is a difference between the top flower and the surrounding ones. It has four petals and eight stamens while the side flowers have five petals and ten stamens. It shoots from a spreading root stock as its flowers seldom culminate in seed. Retiring, gentle, eccentric: its entrusts its seeds to snails. The arrangement of the flowers has been invested with Christian symbolism: they face all directions for Christ's second coming. In the slim shadows cast by Ash, Moschatel can grow in thousands: pale Primroses sit among them while Campion and Sanicle keep underground a while. Though colonies can be very large, sites round here are few.

Moschatel

Another oddity of the early spring is Butcher's-broom; its flower set in the

Butcher's-broom

middle of its "leaf" - not a true leaf, but a flattened stem called a cladode. The queerest lily, living at its northern limit in our Downland woods. In the 19th century Sussex butchers decorated great Christmas sirloins with its berry-laden sprays. It was also used in Christmas wreaths and garlands. In myth, another contender for the Crown of Thorns, *Jew's myrtle* - blood drops running off its spines. Blood runs, too, from the Hazel bud.

Hazel flower

More warmth and light activate not just plants but insects, too. Some are better placed than others to take advantage of the first nectar flow from plants like Dandelion. Only the female bumblebee survives the winter and has now to rear her offspring, but the honeybee is geared to forage as soon as there is sufficient warmth. Then its mighty work begins - it is the most prolific pollinator, far out-doing wasps, bumblebees and butterflies combined. A colony will build its numbers through the spring and might reach 100,000 bees. The worker bees display "plant fidelity" - once a scout bee has done his persuasive waggle-dance indicating a prime nectar site, be it clover or heather as far as two miles away, the foraging bees will restrict their nectar gathering to that site and will fly past other nectar bearing plants. This ensures an efficient delivery of pollen to the correct species. But if other scout bees find a bigger reservoir of nectar or pollen they will persuade foragers into switching their fidelity.

Spring pollen

Alexanders

Never far from the breaking wave, Alexanders spill everywhere. Their leaves, like the Honeysuckle's, brought spring into deep winter's freezing heart. Alexanders were used predominantly as a kitchen herb - *blackpot-herb* - its medical use was quite limited. Shoots, leaves and flowers were cultivated for use in salads, for a vegetable or to be put in broth. It was superseded with the cultivation of celery: left to go wild by the seaside rocks. It may have been an introduction brought to our shores by the Crusaders from Macedonia, home of Alexander the Great - hence its English name. It is aromatic - hence its generic name, Smyrnium. Its fellow is a tiny violet,

the Pale Wood-violet which peppers the grassy banks just short of the sheer white drop. This is an early violet, ahead of the Dog Violet by some weeks.

Pale Wood-violet

Alexanders

Sciophytes, such as Wood Sorrel, are very susceptible to wood clearance, rapidly overcome by heliophytes such as Raspberry and Rosebay Willowherb. And shade there is below the scarp where cloudy ghylls cut shallow channels in the woodland clay. To the sound of slowly running water finely veined Oxalis draws bees and beetles by its nectar. Oddly, these attractive flowers and their pollinators generate little seed. It is a second flush of flowers through the summer, short-stalked flowers which seldom open, that produce the seed. Its sharp-flavoured leaves were popular in salads - indeed it was once cultivated as a salad plant

Wood Sorrel

A sternutatory - juice of its roots "snuffed up the nose occasioned violent sneezing" - a cranial purge - "good for nervous disorders" - the Primrose. Some flowers are born too early for their pollinators: the "pale primroses that die unmarried" as Shakespeare put it. But look

Primrose

Wood Anemone

Cherry Plum

into the muzzle of the primrose and find two kinds of flower - "pin-eyed" and "thrum-eyed" form. The two differ in length of style - this clever design ensures cross-pollination. When the insect pushes in his proboscis he will take pollen from the "thrum" and on his next visit plant it on the "pin". Also, the two kinds of flowers have pollen of different sizes and configurations: only compatible with the stigmas of the opposite kind. Those that flower later can cross with Cowslips to make "false oxlips".

Like the Early Purple Orchid, Wood Anemone is a plant of ancient woodland. Known, too, as the *wind flower,* the whole is poisonous, containing protoanemonine. Paradoxically a decoction of its leaves was used to soothe the skin of lepers, and despite the toxin, pheasants like to eat its flowers. Relatively few pollinating insects are on the wing if March is wintry and, in any case, these flowers hold scant interest as they bear no nectar. Consequently few flowers manage to set seed, and those that ripen may fall on dry leaves where germination is unlikely. For propagation it relies on its creeping root-stock. A gentle plant without petals whose flowers nod when closed: then the pink or lilac sepal-blush is shown.

A mimic of the Sloe's white starry blossom, Cherry Plum breaks while the Blackthorn bud is hidden in the twig.

..... and ever the Yaffle

April

Search carefully and you may find a low arcade which leads deep through the Blackthorn scrub, into a spiny dell. There will likely be a carpet of fresh spring moss and on it a sprinkling of blackthorn petals: wind-blown confetti - a secret place for fairy weddings. Now, the cruel thorns are enveloped in a froth of blossom: the scrub has come alive. After months of "raindrops lingering on the pointed thorn" the sloes light up the slopes and crown the tops of Downland. Brown Hairstreak, distinctive "tails" on hind wings, will sip on honeydew and lay its eggs on Blackthorn twigs. The young Blackthorn leaves, yet to appear, will be the caterpillars' food. Blossom on a bare twig can be heart-achingly beautiful. These dark stems throw out clouds that sparkle white and drift like mist across the landscape. As the blossoms age, reluctant leaves push through, and, slowly the scrub will turn a smoky green. A useful plant, but one unlucky in the house. Sloe for jams and gin and the likely forerunner to the garden plum and greengage. Called *winter picks* in Sussex, their juice was used as a gargle for sore gums and "a means of fastening loose

Blackthorn

teeth" [C]. The flowers were for colic and its bark powdered for a febrifuge. Its magic also worked on warts - "stick a snail upon a Blackthorn and the warts will waste". For the honeybee, an early source of nectar and of pollen if conditions are suitable for the bees to fly.

Green and white are the defining colours of our landscape through spring and early summer. Blackthorn first, then the Wayfaring Tree, then Cow Parsley, followed on by Hawthorn. Cow Parsley boils up on roadside verges and edges yellow fields of Rape. Grand under a cloudless sky, but see it too, once the sun is down by light of moon - white plants like Yarrow and Wild Parsley reward a moonlit journey on the chalk - indeed in Wiltshire they call it *moonlight*. This is the earliest of the hedgebank umbellifers, leaves first showing at the winter solstice. However dainty,

Spindle Wood

Cow Parsley

however light, it was associated with the Devil: "Deil's meal" in Scotland - very likely for its resemblance to its cousin Hemlock.

Lords-and-Ladies, *Parson in the Pulpit,* grows "in shadowie places" as

Lords-and-ladies

Gerard noted, often under the elder or guarded by a snarl of bramble. The flowers are enveloped by a spathe, or hood - "like the ear of an hare" [(G)]. Tucked well down is a ring of male flowers and at the very base a mass of larger female flowers. Its spadix, a purple flower-bearing spike, heats up and exudes a foetid scent attracting small insects, such as Owl Midges, which are trapped by an array of stiff down-pointing hairs. Only when these hairs wither can the pollen-laden insects go free. Its starchy rhizome was used as a thickener, like cornflower today, in cookery. Culpeper knew it as *starch-wort.* For him it was a "sure remedy for the plague", and he noted how "the country people about Maidstone use the herbe and root instead of soap". A sexual plant, *priest's pintle,* the spike within the hood, subversive, authority brought down, a *devil's finger,* the priest fighting his own sexuality. Pint is likely a contraction of pintle, or penis, cuckoo perhaps signifying vigour and lust, perhaps relating to the sorry cuckold. In Kent it had a gentle sexuality - *kitty-come-down-the-lane-and-jump-up-and-kiss-me.* Gerard was practical and knew how its starch was "most hurtfull for the hands of the laundress that hath the handling of it, for it choppeth, blistereth and maketh the hands rough and rugged and withal smarting". The fiery taste of its root is lost after drying and powdering, and it was used as a

Cow Parsley

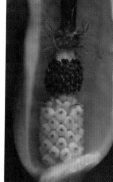

inside the spathe

Ramsons

Blackthorn

Early Purple Orchids

Red Campion and Ramsons

Early Purple Orchid

Garlic Mustard

Goldilocks Buttercup

kind of arrowroot flour. As much of the refining was done in Portland the product was sold in London as Portland Sago - a food for invalids.

Badger's flower fits well, hinting at seclusion - a world in twilight or in darkness where the coppice floor is flooded with reflected light, white as the badgers stripe picked out by the rays from the far-off moon. Bruised, it becomes the *stink plant* or *gipsy's onions.* The sulphur-containing chemicals it emits evolved as a deterrent to voracious herbivores. Here and there a clump of Bluebells or a stand of *Weasel's-snout* rise from the Ramson floor. At the woodland edge, pinked up with Campion, a crumbling chalky bank is where the breaking wave of ramsons hits the hard flint track. Gerard encouraged the use of the leaf in fish sauce but otherwise found little practical application for it. Its species name, ursinum, - Latin ursus, a bear - might have been suggested by the similarity of its leaves to bears' ears. Alternatively it suggests its inferiority to cultivated garlic - fit only for bears; like a dog plant - fit only

for dogs. The only British cabbage that smells of garlic is the Garlic Mustard - all other garlicky plants are of the lily family. Also a condiment and put with fish - a *poor man's mustard* or *sauce alone.* Gerard recommended it particularly with salt fish. While Garlic Mustard is plentiful, unfortunately salt fish, a delicacy from my Highland childhood, is not easily come by in these Southern parts. In June the pale green caterpillar of the Orange Tip butterfly feeds off the same coloured seed-pods. Shiny leafed and bright of flower, happy in the April hedgebank.

In the leaf mould, by Moschatel and Early Purple Orchid, you may chance upon Goldilocks, the woodland buttercup. It has a worn appearance as if pecked out by birds. Of the two varieties one is apetalous, it is the sepals that are crinkled yellow.

Ash buds, now black and velvety, will later split open and put out leaves tinged a peculiar sooty green. But

Ash buds

first the ash will flower. At first glance this strange

purple flower resembles a resin that has oozed and bubbled from the bark. Ash flowers are usually bisexual, that is male and female parts are produced together. However, some trees are single sex. The strangest thing is that such a tree can, from year to year ,change its sex, first producing all male flowers, subsequently all female flowers. Ash burns well, and even "in the green" it will not spit or spark. It fed the fire by which Mary gave new-born Christ His first wash. Strong and pliant, it had endless agricultural uses, made into tool handles, carts and oars. Unfortunately, it is not suitable for fencing as it rots too quickly in the ground. It was commonly planted in hedgerows with a view to future use. The ideal wood for a shepherd's crook - folklore had it that the Ash was incapable of harming stock. A tree with apotropaic powers - "in many parts of the Highlands, nurse or midwife at the birth of a child, ... puts one end of a green stick of this tree into the fire and, while it is burning, receives into a spoon the sap or juice which oozes out at the other end, and administers this as the first spoonful of liquor to the new-born babe" - imbuing the babe with strength and protecting it from evil. Gilbert White in the "Natural History and Antiquities of Selbourne" described the use of the Ash in curing children of rupture. It was also used to treat rickets - the Ash was cleft open with Oak wedges and the affected child passed through the cleft. The tree was then "plastered with loam and carefully swathed up". As the tree healed, so too the child. Gilbert White also described the "shrew-ash". Shrews were believed to run over cattle and bring them illness. The treatment was complicated - first a hole was bored in an Ash tree into which a living shrew was introduced and subsequently entombed. Ultimately the stroke of a branch taken from that tree could heal affected beasts.

Where the fulmars nest on the bare chalk faces of Beachy Head Wallflowers peek from arid salt-caked

Cliff-side Wallflower

Painted Lady on Wallflower

Lady's Smock

Scurvy-grass

fissures. Edward Whimper, the conqueror of the Matterhorn, with his brother - "schoolboys with the impudence of ignorance" - had tried to scale the great chalk cliff, the Devil's chimney. He later said "we have often been in danger of different kinds but have never more nearly broken our necks". In this harsh environment this unassuming flower has found a bastion. Painted Lady, like the Red Admiral and the Clouded Yellow, is a migrant - crossing mountain range and sea to reach our Downland - from the desert margins of the Atlas mountains. In 2003 there had been an

White Dead-nettle

enormous influx. They arrived early, too, at the very beginning of June and then by 3rd June they were seen in Inverness and a few days later in the Shetland Isles. Further west and very local in the coastal shingle is the Scurvy-grass. Elsewhere it is common-or-garden, as in the Scillies where in early spring its white corymbs throw ribbons that curve along the foreshore. James Lind, a Scottish naval surgeon, in 1753 published "A Treatise of the Scurvy". He approached the problem of scurvy in a scientific way, comparing various treatments in a controlled trial done at sea on board a naval vessel called the Salisbury. Sailors given two oranges and a lemon every day recovered from the scurvy dramatically more quickly than those on any other treatment. Scurvy, a vitamin C deficiency syndrome, was a problem for the land-locked populace as well as the seafarer, but long voyages of the 16th century brought it wider recognition. The most characteristic feature was swelling and sponginess of the gums, so called "scurvy buds". The teeth eventually loosened and fell out. Large spontaneous bruises would arise, usually in the legs, producing the characteristic "woody leg". Fresh wounds failed to

Ground Ivy

heal, and severe cases could die suddenly of heart failure. In Vasco da Gama's epic voyage round the Cape of Good Hope in 1497 one hundred of his one hundred and sixty crew died of scurvy. Herbalists, having discovered the anti-scorbutic effect of Cochlearia officinalis, raised it in the physic garden. Cochlearia anglica was not so easily cultivated so herb women collected it for the apothecaries from the Thames-side creeks and flats. The dried herb, or a bottled distillation, was taken aboard for long voyages and, ultimately, it became fashionable to take a glass of scurvy-grass water every morning, rather as we now take orange juice.

Even in the early nineteenth century scurvy-grass sandwiches were eaten. A lilac crucifer with a very high vitamin C content is Lady's Smock with its four pale petals, and a companion to the Primrose. "Devil's saliva" hangs upon its stem - indicating the presence of the Meadow Froghopper's larvae. The Orange Tip also feeds off its freely running nectar. Lady's Smock's main requirement is moist ground, but for its friend the Primrose soil type is the main factor in governing its distribution - it abhors dry chalk.

Some plants belie their mundane names. The *White Bee-nettle* is better fitted for this exotic than drear Dead-nettle. It guards its nectar closely - fenced off by a row of hairs, lying at the bottom of the corolla tube, kept safe for pollinators. Its white flesh is soft-tinged with the merest green. Turn it upside down and see *Adam-and-Eve-in-the-Bower.*

Green Alkanet

Dog Violet

Hairy Violet

Greater Celandine

Ground Ivy will bloom on till summer is far spent, but now early Brimstones flit about its purply mats. Otherwise known as *gill,* its leaves were used by brewers as a bitter and to clarify their beers: hence gill ale. In the 17th century beer was also tunned up with other additives to enhance its effect - notable amongst them was "mad-honey". This hallucinogenic honey - deli bali - is still produced by Turkish beekeepers farming bees on Rhododendron ponticum on the slopes that rise from the Black Sea coast and can be bought from under the counter. Andromedotoxin from its nectar makes a poisonous honey - lethal if too much is taken. Both Culpeper and Gerard were strong proponents of Ground Ivy. The former used it for a gargle and for a wound cleanser - "excellent to wash sores and ulcers in the privy parts of man or woman", "doth wonderfully cleanse fistulas" while Gerard stuffed it into ears for the "humming noyse". He also noted its veterinary application: its juice, run out by stamping, mixed with ale and honey, then squirted into the animal's inflamed eye.

Perhaps Green Alkanet is native in Devon and Cornwall but otherwise it is an introduction from France in the Middle Ages. A dye plant, named from the Arabic alhenna or "henna shrub" which yielded a red dye, still used by women in the Near East to decorate their nails and hair. Here it is frequent around the Downland villages but never far from habitation. It has settled in

Early Spider Orchid

some chalk pits but is more than likely "over-the-garden-wall".

Like Sweet Violet, Dog Violet sometimes bears cleistogamic flowers - inconspicuous flowers which are never open and which self-fertilise. Otherwise, its scentless flowers are usually blue-violet with a pale, if not whitish, spur. Formerly the flowers were powdered and used to treat quinsy and the pleurisy, while the leaves were "fried with the yolks of egg" and applied directly to piles. Its leaves are plentiful in the close-grazed turf. By the sea, chalk grassland is the place for Viola hirta, the Hairy Violet. Sometimes blossoming in early March, it lacks the runners and the scent of sweet violet and is rather paler than the dog violet. Greater Celandine, too, was widely used medicinally, indeed grown for its toxic orange sap.

Hunched and hardly off the turf, late April sees the first of the Early Spider Orchids. Some grow on track ways where, sadly, they are likely to be trampled - indeed ancient tracks are a favoured habitat. Those that flower later and hide amongst the Bulbous Buttercups do better. Whin's yellow rarely touches the white cliff edge: more usually it is the yellow of Mignonette and Weld. Yet more yellow

breaks out as the month goes by: vast sheets of nectar-laden Oilseed Rape which is extensively farmed on Downland slopes. Important to the beekeeper, albeit a headache in the extraction of its quick-setting honey.

Narrow tracks made by sheep and cows wend up slopes where Cowslips crowd. The trembling of the Cowslips signified a wort for diseases of the nervous system - not just for tremor but for the 'falling sickness', pains in the nerves, false apparitions and paralysis to name but a few of the 'infirmities' of the brain - hence it was also known as *palsywort*.

I like to go among them on the northern slopes, zigzag, drawn by this track then that, moving slowly through them. Named from the cow pat whence it sprang, it also had a close association with St Peter - *herb Peter, keys-of-heaven* and *St Peter's keys*. According to legend the first cowslip grew where St Peter dropped the keys to heaven - a piece of heaven we are grateful for.

..... *and ever the Yaffle*

Cowslips

...and May in prospect

Index

Bibliography

Akeroyd, J.	*The Encylopedia of Wild Flowers,* 1999
Brandon, P.	*The Sussex Landscape,* 1974
Coulcher, P.	*A Natural History of the Cuckmere Valley,* 1997
Culpeper, N.	*Complete Herbal,* 1653, ed. Manchester 1826, Rev.
Garrard, I., Streeter, D.	*The Wild Flowers of the British Isles,* 1983
Gerard, J.	*The Herball or Generall Historie of Plantes,* 1597
Grant, I. F.	*Highland Folkways,* 1995
Grigson, G.	*The Englishman's Flora,* 1955
Howes, F. N.	*Plants and Beekeeping,* 1979
Hudson, W. H.	*Nature in Downland,* 1900
Lang, D.	*Wild Orchids of Sussex,* 2001
Martin, W. K.	*Over the Hills,* 1968
Martin, W. K.	*The Concise British Flora in Colour,* 1965
Morton, H. V.	*Through Lands of the Bible,* 1938
Pechey, J.	*The Compleat Herbal of Physical Plants,* 1694
Porter, V.	*The Southdown Sheep,* 1991
Reader's Digest	*Britain's Wildlife, Plants and Flowers,* 1987
Turner, W.	*Names of Herbes,* 1549, ed. Britten, J. 1892
Turrill, W. R.	*British Plant Life,* 1989
Whalley, P.	*Butterfly Watching,* 1980
White, G.	*Natural History and Antiquities of Selbourne,* 1789
Willis, B.	*Shepherds of Sussex,* 2000
Withering, W.	*Botanical Arrangement of British Plants,* 1796

About the Author

William N Macleod spent his childhood in the Scottish Highlands, his parents hailing from the Isle of Lewis, and the Orkney Isles. In 1990 he left Scotland for Sussex and discovered the gentle beauty of the Downs. He lives in Eastbourne with his wife and two children and works as a consultant neurologist.

In his spare time he enjoys beekeeping, historic rally-driving, wind-surfing and wild-trout fishing.